MW00480241

"Few would argue that as Christians, we bear the responsibility to protect, both in a spiritual and physical sense. In "Concealed Carry for Christians," author Skip Coryell lays the foundation for believers developing both the mental and spiritual mindset needed to carry a defensive firearm on a daily basis, while exploring tough questions about how far the call to "be your brother's keeper" extends when it comes to matters of life and death. Coryell effectively makes the case that it's ok for Christians to have the mindset of a warrior, but effective warriors like the Biblical David are created through a lifetime dedication to training along with deep faith in Christ. The author correctly acknowledges that in addition to physical and mental training needed to effectively and responsibly carry a firearm, the most important aspect is spiritual fitness. A true warrior and protector must have a deep personal relationship with the living Savior and leave the house each day with all their "I love you's" said to family members, in case this is the day a complete sacrifice must be made in defense of others. Coryell carries the justification for protection to establishing safety and security teams, both armed and unarmed, for houses of worship, touching on risks from adverse weather, medical emergencies and lost children on up to mass casualty events."

–John McLaughlin
Church Safety, Security Team Consultant

ACTIVE SELF

PROTECTION
ATTITUDE . SKILLS . PLAN

"Christians have wrestled with the idea of self-defense since not long after the church was founded, and we've asked questions about whether and how we can protect ourselves from criminal violence. I am grateful to Skip for tackling these tough issues with class, with grace, and with thoughtfulness. If you're a follower of Jesus you'll enjoy this read!"

John Correia
Active Self Protection

As we put on the armor of God according to Ephesians 6:11 "Put on the whole armour of God, that ye may be able to stand against the wiles of the devil". Let Skip arm you with knowledge, skill, and love so that you can be prepared to fight the enemy in your daily walk. You will learn how to be armed physically, emotionally, and spiritually.

Be safe and Be Blessed
Terry L. Johnson, Esq.
Attorney and friend

Contents

Disclaimer

The information in this book is, in the opinion of the author, sound tactical advice. However, please take the information in this book with a healthy level of skepticism. Don't do something that doesn't make sense to you. Additionally, the author is not a theologian, neither is he licensed to practice law in any jurisdiction. Before incorporating any information in this book into your life, you should consult a competent, licensed legal and/or tactical professional. This book is intended to compliment formal training with a firearms instructor - it does not replace it. Your training is not sufficient without personal range instruction from a competent, certified firearms instructor.

ISBN 978-1-61808-147-6

Printed in the United States of America

White Feather Press

Reaffirming Faith in God, Family, and Country!

Books by Skip Coryell

We Hold These Truths

Bond of Unseen Blood

Church and State

Blood in the Streets

Laughter and Tears

RKBA: Defending the Right to Keep and Bear Arms

Stalking Natalie

The God Virus

The Shadow Militia

The Saracen Tide

The Blind Man's Rage

Civilian Combat - The Concealed Carry Book

Jackpine Strong

Concealed Carry for Christians

I dedicate this book to my wife and children ... the reason I train and carry.

In memory of Larry Jackson

friend

warrior

Concealed Carry for Christians

Encouragement for the

Armed Christian

Skip

Coryell

Foreword

I grew up in a church-going home with a dad who never owned a gun; we had BB guns in our home, and dad would hang burnt-out light bulbs in a box and let me shoot at them with my BB gun. In high school I took Army ROTC where I was exposed to all kinds of firearms and trained to shoot a .22 rifle. Then I went to West Point and joined the Army. I had very little training in shooting—and then I got to Vietnam. During my first tour I was a rifle platoon leader; during my second tour I was a rifle company commander. My job wasn't to shoot, but to direct the employment (and shooting) of my soldiers. Yes, there were times when I did shoot, but they were rare. In my entire life I had never been attacked or hurt—a good part of that, during my adult life was because I was a 6'3" army ranger and I knew how to take on the "air" that says "you don't want to mess with me."

Then, as a civilian, I realized that there were bad people out there who could hurt me and my family—and those around me. So, I purchased a firearm—a revolver. I was smart enough to know that I had to learn how to use it, so I had friends take me to the range and had me practice. I wasn't great, but I was good. I got my concealed pistol permit and continued to practice.

This made me aware how vulnerable my church was—with some 3000 attendees. I spoke to my church leadership but got nowhere. I struggled with all of the issues Skip covers in *Concealed Carry for Christians*. I had already, as a soldier, concluded that the Bible in no way prohibits killing—no where in the Bible did anyone tell soldiers to abandon their duties. Indeed, in the Ten Commandments a proper translation would say "Thou shalt not murder," while some translations inappropriately say "Thou shalt not kill." Much to my delight, my church began an armed Church Safety Team several years ago; I serve on it.

It's very clear that we have an obligation to resist evil in all its forms—and that certainly includes evil people who are predators. Skip does an excellent job speaking of all the ways individuals and families can be attacked. Yes, prayer works—but faith without works is dead. Recent church shootings make this clear.

Skip's advice about avoiding bad circumstances and people is just common sense. This will reduce the chances of an evil situation—but bad things do happen and being prepared is the only solution—the only Christian solution. I hope I never have a reason to fire my weapon in civilian life, but I will be ready should that day come.

I strongly recommend *Concealed Carry for Christians* to everyone—and especially to all Christians. Even if you plan to never own a firearm, you'll be glad you read this book.

Denny Gillem
Lieutenant Colonel, US Army (Ret)
Author, The Smiling Ranger

From the Author

I started carrying a pistol almost twenty years ago, and I've been a member of a church safety team for about 15 years now. The church safety team is like other ministries in that we are serving the body of Christ, but there is one very distinct and important difference. It might get you killed.

I've been a Sunday school teacher, even Sunday School Superintendant. I've served on musical teams. I've been an usher. I've even helped in the children's ministry where they expected me to dance up and down to silly songs while making ridiculous hand motions. (Thank God there are no existing pictures for that one. It wasn't pretty.)

However, none of those jobs ever required me to take a bullet for the flock. As a Sunday School teacher I was never expected to run towards gunshots while drawing my firearm. Most Sunday School teachers don't carry pepper spray; they don't practice open-handed skills to become proficient at taking a man to the ground and putting him in zip ties. They are not trained in the subtle arts of interrogation and visually identifying physical threats, like who is armed and who is not.

It's a different kind of ministry, requiring a different kind of Christian. However, all these concerns are not restricted to the church safety team, because they apply to any Christian who decides to carry a gun.

If you are considering carrying a gun or joining a church safety team, then, this book is a must-read for you. You should not go into the job lightly, as there are many things to consider.

1. Can you take a human life? Killing a fellow human being is not and should not be a natural and easy

thing to do. It should be tough. It may take years of prayer and study and self-reflection before you decide the answer.

2. Do you want to carry a gun? It's a nuisance, a total life change and a bona fide pain in the butt. Carrying a gun dictates every facet of your life: how you treat others, what you wear, how you talk and how you walk. It's not for everyone.

3. Are you willing to die to protect the ones you love? How about strangers? Will you die to protect someone you haven't even met yet.

4. Are you willing to spend lots of time and money on training and equipment? Less than one percent of the concealed carry population ever go on to take training that is not required by the government. That statistic should scare you.

Buying a gun doesn't make you a gun fighter any more than buying a guitar makes you a rock star. We are called by God to excellence in everything we do. The gun is a powerful tool. The sacrifice you make could be supreme. It is a life-or-death decision.

This book was written to empower and encourage Christians who decide to carry concealed. You are an elite corps of individuals. You are warriors. Welcome to the club!

Skip Coryell

Joshua 1:9 (NIV)

Have I not commanded you? Be strong and courageous. Do not be afraid; do not be discouraged, for the Lord your God will be with you wherever you go."

Chapter 1

Courageous

WHEN **I** THINK ABOUT IT, REALLY think about it, the one movie that has affected me in the most positive way is the 2011 movie by the Kendricks brothers called *Courageous*. I can still remember watching it for the first time, how I cried like a baby, how it silenced me before God and my family, how it moved me to change, to improve, to work harder and to take my responsibility as a father and a husband to a new level.

Now, sure, I'd always taken parenthood seriously, knew that being a dad and husband was one of the most important things I'd ever do, but ... the movie, the experience, is what inspired me to actually get out there and do my job better. There is something magical about the power of a good story. To the human soul, it inspires us, imbues us with power and courage and love.

And then there's that title song by the group *Casting*

Crowns. The first line of that song is an incredible epiphany to me.

> *We were made to be courageous.*
> *We were made to lead the way.*

What does that really mean? Here's how I break it down for myself.

1. <u>We were made.</u>

> *Psalm 139:14 (NIV)*
> *I praise you because I am fearfully*
> *and wonderfully made; your works are*
> *wonderful, I know that full well.*

The Bible is clear throughout, from the very beginning, that we are not pond scum; we were not cosmic accidents; we didn't accidentally happen when a few enzymes and chemicals mixed together of their own accord and were zapped with electricity. We didn't just "happen." We were created, wonderfully made. And we were made by God, the most powerful force in the universe. Doesn't that knowledge change you? Encourage you? Humble you?

There is no stamp on your forehead that says "Made in China." The stamp is on our souls, and it says "Made by God ... in His image."

> *So God created mankind in his own image,*
> *in the image of God he created them; male*
> *and female he created them.*
>
> *Genesis 1:27 (NIV)*

2. <u>We were made ... to be courageous.</u>

And, if we were made, not an accident, but fearfully and wonderfully made, by an intelligent, benevolent being, then ...

it stands to reason that we were also made for a purpose. After all, why would an intelligent, reasoning, loving and logical God create other beings without purpose? We find over and over again, by looking at the world around us, that people without purpose are driven to madness and depression, even terrible acts of violence, such as suicide and mass shootings. And what is that purpose? Why did God create us?

> God made you to be courageous and to lead the way.

Think about your reasons for becoming a parent, and it may become clear to you. You created your children, so you'd have someone to love. God created His children so He could love us as well. If we can love our own children, with all our flaws and shortcomings, then how much more magnificent is God's love for His children? For us. All of us.

God made us to be many things, but the one thing this song reveals is this. God made us to be courageous. We were fearfully and wonderfully made in God's image. Do you really believe that God is afraid; that he's a coward; that He prowls the universe in the shadows, hides from danger, going out of His way to mind His own business, selfishly doing only what is in His own best interest. If that were true, we never would have been created.

I know that I disappointed my parents from time to time. I know there were times they may have asked the question "Why did I create that boy?" My own children have disappointed me at times. But I still love them, and I will still die for them if that's what's needed to save them.

But God demonstrates his own love for us in

3

> *this: While we were still sinners, Christ died*
> *for us.*

Romans 5:8 (NIV)

3. <u>We were made to lead the way</u>.

Think about the people in the Bible that you respect, re-vere and admire. Is it Judas, who betrayed Christ? Is it King Herod, filled with greed? Is it Pharaoh, hardhearted and ar-rogant? The obvious answer is no.

We admire Joshua for his courage. We admire Paul for his steadfast resolution. We admire Moses because, despite his fear, he obeyed God and stood up to the most powerful king-dom of his time.

We were made to be courageous, because God admires courage. All these people we revere and admire were leaders, people who, despite their fear, chose to obey God rather than men. They were brave men who stood up against the evil of the world to lead the way.

Fear is a prerequisite to courage. Without fear there can be no bravery. Fear is the thing we overcome. We were made by God to be overcomers, to be leaders, to be ... courageous.

> *When you go to war against your enemies*
> *and see horses and chariots and an army*
> *greater than yours, do not be afraid of them,*
> *because the Lord your God, who brought*
> *you up out of Egypt, will be with you.*

Deuteronomy 20:1 (NIV)

In the movie, *Courageous*, the men of God take a resolu-tion before God and their families, promising many virtuous things. I took that pledge as well, in front of God, in front of my family, and I signed it. Now, it sits on my desk, staring at me, reminding me of who God wants me to be.

The very first line reads as follows:

> *I do solemnly resolve before God to take full responsibility for myself, my wife, and my children.*

That is huge. Full responsibility is a lot; it's all encompassing, leaving nothing good to chance. You have a duty to protect your family, and I'm not talking about just the men here ... but also you women as well. When evil comes knockin' the parents get rockin.' That's the way it has to be for the family to survive and even flourish.

And that evil can take many forms. It could be the person holding a knife against your wife's throat. It could be the pedophile who is trying to hurt your children. It could be the hormone-laden, selfish teenage boy who wants to sully your daughter's good name. Another promise in the *Courageous* pledge reads as follows:

> *I WILL love them, protect them, serve them, and teach them the Word of God as the spiritual leader of my home.*

To love .. is also to ... protect.

We naturally want to protect the ones we love. And that protection requires courage. It's one of our parental tools, and it's every bit as important as the gun I carry on my belt. The challenge with the gun, is it will not always be with you.

You are commissioned by God to protect your family whether you are armed or open-handed. Because of the myriad of laws that criss-cross our nation, you may be disarmed from time to time. But the three things you will always have is your courage, your faith in God, and your love for your spouse and children.

I'm reminded of a quote from the 1991 movie, *Robin Hood: Prince of Thieves*, that inspired me as well. There was an exchange between Robin Hood (played by Kevin Costner) and Will Scarlett (played by Christian Slater) where Will asks Robin:

> *"What would you have us do, fight armored men on horseback with rocks and bare hands?"*

> *"If needs be. But with the one true weapon that escapes you, Will. Courage."*

Courage can always be with you. It's your birthright before God, but you must choose to accept it and exercise it.

Now, I know many of you might be thinking how naive I am right now, saying, "But Skip, you don't know the life I've lived, how hard it's been for me."

> **Courage is not passed on through your bloodline. You have to earn it with your actions.**

Well, that may not be true. My life has been a bit rocky as well, and I view myself as a chain breaker. When first starting out, I had very humble beginnings. My parents were poor, my father a factory worker. His own parents were of World War One and depression-era vintage. My grandfather was an almost lifelong alcoholic, and I'm sure that affected my own father. We all affect our children, for good or ill. But I recall the one thing my father said to me that molded me more than any other, "Son, the best part of you went running down your mother's leg."

That pronouncement of my father forged chains around my heart that I've struggled to break for decades now. But it was a curse that only God could break. And God did break that curse.

When I started life, I had grand and glorious dreams for myself. I was going to write the all-American novel, win the Pulitzer prize, become famous and rich. That didn't happen.

> I exist to protect my children, not just physically, but spiritually as well.

However, I did work hard to break the curse for my children. Here's one thing I've learned: my true legacy, isn't in the books I write, or the radio shows I produce; it's in the way that I live my life in front of my children for all to see. A man's true legacy is in living a life for Christ, having faith in God and obeying His commands. I live my life to break the chains and free my children.

I exist to protect my children, not just physically, but also spiritually. I model, as best I can, faith and love in God. If you've had a rough past, that doesn't rule out a beautiful future, serving God and the ones you love. But the one thing you'll need to be successful in life, and the thing you'll need to pass on to your kids is courage.

No matter what happens in life, no matter how discouraged you get ... you'll need courage. Notice that the words "courage" and "discourage" are very similar but have opposite meanings.

Always remember that we were not made by God to be discouraged. We were made to be courageous.

The last line in that song by *Casting Crowns* is this:

> *"Seek Justice, Love Mercy, Walk humbly*
> *with our God."*

To do that you'll need courage, self-sacrifice and, above all, love for the ones you are sworn to protect. If you haven't yet heard the song *Courageous* by the group *Casting Crowns*, then please do so now. And if you haven't viewed the movie *Courageous* by Stephen and Alex Kendrick, then drop everything you're doing right now and get it done.

It will change you and your children ... forever.

Things to Remember

1. You bear the primary responsibility for protecting and defending your family.

2. Courage is not a birthright. You have to earn it with your acts of bravery.

3. You were fearfully and wonderfully made ... to be courageous.

4. Our courage and our strength come from God.

Job 14:11-13 (NIV)

11 As the water of a lake dries up or a riverbed becomes parched and dry, 12 so he lies down and does not rise; till the heavens are no more, people will not awake or be roused from their sleep.

Chapter 2

Wakin' Up is Hard to Do!

MY WIFE GETS UP ALMOST EVERY day at 5AM with a song in her heart and a smile on her face. She puts on a pot of coffee, then gets on the treadmill and works out. From there she comes back upstairs and studies her Bible for about forty-five minutes. Sara is a paragon of virtue, hard work and consistency. You've heard that old army commercial that says "We do more by 9AM than most people do all day!"

My wife is like that. Me? Not so much. Okay, I'll be honest. That's not like me at all. I am not a morning person. Lord knows I've tried to keep her schedule, but ... it's to no avail. My mind seems to come alive after darkness falls, teeming with new ideas, bulging with plot lines to stories, racing faster than Mario Andretti on the final lap.

I don't even set my alarm clock on most days. I wake up when something wakes me up. Sometimes it's a crash; sometimes it's a scream; sometimes it's a kid shaking me saying "Daddy, are you awake?"

I'm reminded of that old Neil Sedaka song titled "Breakin' up is Hard to do." I love the song; it came out in 1975, my senior year in high school. But since then I've altered the words a little. It's still a beautiful love song, but ... I don't know ... through the years the object of my love has changed slightly. At 61 years of age, I'm now singing a different tune.

> Don't take your '*sleep*' away from me
> Don't you leave my heart in misery
> If you go then I'll be blue
> 'Cause '*waking*' up is hard to do

> On average, humans sleep for 25 years; that's one-third of their lives.

You see ... I'm in love with sleep.

I love slumber. I love sloth. I love to wake up at 9AM and then close my eyes and go back to sleep. Why? I don't know. I suppose I do it because I can. For 25 years I worked in the corporate rat race and had to get up every morning early, before it was light outside, before I wanted to, before I even had a pulse. In the morning hours my blood runs thick and heavy like cold molasses, sometimes stopping altogether to rest while I sleep. I don't even have a heartbeat until 10AM.

But I still get plenty of work done. Some nights I can't sleep until most people are getting up. So ... I drag my butt out of bed and I write. You might say it's my way of making up for lost time.

I beg of you don't say goodbye
Can't we give our '*rest*' another try?
Come on, baby, let's start anew
'Cause '*waking*' up is hard to do

I understand the temptation to be lazy, I really do. I understand that it's much easier to just leave the trash sitting there than it is to drag the dumpster to the curb, but ... I also know that bad things can happen if I refuse to wake up. My wife will get mad at me. My kids will know that Dad's a sloth and emulate my poor behavior. There are lots of reasons to get up in the morning. I'll get more work done and pay my bills. I'll be healthier.

Only 21% of Americans get the recommended 7 to 8 hours sleep per night.

But still ... wakin' up ... is hard, so very hard ... to do.

So by now you must be asking, "Why are you sharing this with us?" Well, because it's germane to our discussion on personal defense. Allow me to explain.

Every week I take phone calls and emails and text messages and FaceBook private messages from people who tell me they want to take a concealed carry class but ... and then they tell me why they can't.

- My wife won't let me
- I don't have time
- I don't have a gun
- I can't get Saturdays off
- I don't have the money

- The government shouldn't require it anyway
- I'm not a good enough shot yet
- The stars aren't properly aligned
- It's too cold
- It's too hot
- It's too nice out

> **Humans are the only mammals who delay sleep.**

It seems there are as many excuses as there are people on the planet. But here's what I think. Most people don't really believe that anything bad will ever happen to them. They are asleep in their cocoons; safely nestled away, snug as a bug in a rug. And I understand that. I get it. Because, let's be honest here. Most of us aren't going to be mugged today. Very few of us will be heinously and viciously stabbed to death. Only a small percentage of women will be raped this week. Only a few men will be shot. Most of us won't be carjacked.

The vast majority of us will wake up in the morning, get ready for work, stop off for coffee before heading into the office, and then we'll work all day in a secure, locked-down facility. And then ... we'll come home and watch television inside a house with an alarm system, go to bed, sleep, then wake up the next day and do it all over again.

Life is good. Until ... life is bad.

I was teaching a concealed carry class in Iowa a long time ago, when a woman in class broke down and started to cry. She ran out of the room and locked herself in the bathroom.

I kept teaching for about ten minutes, but it was hard because the bathroom wasn't sound proof and the whole class could hear her wailing away in agony. I knew that she was okay physically, so I kept teaching until it became too distracting, and then finally gave every one a break until she came back out. And then we got to talking.

She had been meaning to take the class for a long time, but the time just never seemed to be right. Other things always took precedent, because, she knew that she'd make it through the day without a carry permit and a gun.

Then one day she was attacked and severely beaten and raped by her ex-husband. She woke up. Suddenly, getting personal defense training and carrying a gun became a priority to her. She didn't want it to ever happen again. Unfortunately, she would be forced to live with the emotional scars

> The average person falls asleep in seven minutes.

for the rest of her life. I applaud her decision to come to class and get trained and armed, but ... I just wish ... she'd done it sooner, before the milk had been spilled.

So many of us think that nothing bad will ever happen to us. True, a few of us will lead what appears to be charmed lives; however, most of us will not. Here's the bottom line folks: If you live long enough, something bad will happen to you. Evil exists, and some day evil will visit your door. The only question to ask yourself is; Will I be ready? For most people the answer is no. While still others think they're ready and they're not.

Now, I understand why many people do this. They know they are sheep; that they are helpless to defend themselves. But if they admit that the world is unsafe, that there are wolves out there, then they are in danger and must either make a change or live in fear. Most people are lazy. They don't want to wake up. They want to lay in bed, or in the recliner and watch television or the football game. But is that really what's best for you and your family? I think not.

"Arise, take up your bed, and walk."

But hey, Com, comma, do down, down. It's just too hard to wake up. It's painful. It's uncomfortable. It doesn't feel good and I don't like it!

> Women sleep more than men, because their brains work harder, due to multi-tasking.

Yep. I know. But life isn't fair. I so much wish that the world was full of good guys and girls who always played nice and treated each other with kindness and generosity.

But ... well, you already know what I'm going to say. So, I'll shut up. In a minute.

But please don't take our love away from me. Please don't shoot the messenger. Don't get mad and throw it all away. Can't we just try our love one more time?

Cuz wakin' up baby, is hard, so very hard, to do.

If you have a loved one who refuses to wake up; they are in danger. Pray for them. Then go talk to them and tell them how much you care about them; that you don't want to see them get hurt.

You may not talk them into getting armed and trained, but ... maybe you can heighten their state of situational awareness. Maybe you can plant a warrior seed deep inside them that could possibly sprout in the spring. Who knows. It could happen. Remember, most of personal protection has nothing to do with a firearm. The first step is waking up and smelling the evil.

And then while you're at it, put your hands together and clap to get a good rhythm going, then move your feet and your hips a bit while you sing with me and Neal Sedaka and the down dooby doo down down song.

And always remember, wakin' up is hard to do, but if you don't do it ...

You just might be caught off guard and go down dooby doo down down ... for a very long time.

From God's Word

Psalm 139:18 (NLT) *I can't even count them; they outnumber the grains of sand! And when I wake up, you are still with me!*

Proverbs 6:9 (NLT) *But you, lazybones, how long will you sleep? When will you wake up?*

Romans 13:11 (NLT) *This is all the more urgent, for you know how late it is; time is running out. Wake up, for our salvation is nearer now than when we first believed.*

John 4:35 (NLT) *You know the saying, 'Four months between planting and harvest.' But I say, wake up and look around. The fields are already ripe for harvest.*

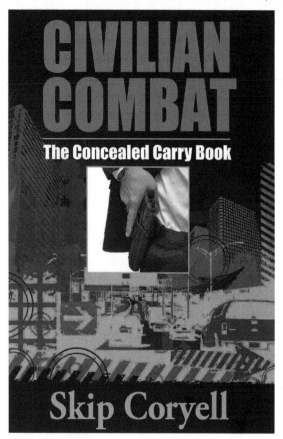

More and more people across the country are seeing the dangers in society and deciding to carry concealed to protect themselves and their families. Skip's book lays it out step by step, teaching you how to protect and defend the ones you love. Read his book and get the benefit of his 19 years of teaching experience and his lifetime of training for this important role in society. *Civilian Combat* is also a great teaching tool for other concealed carry instructors as well. It's a complete curriculum with a final test as well as important points to remember and a list of excellent resources in your journey to personal and family protection.

Proverbs 13:20 (NIV)

Walk with the wise and become wise, for a companion of fools suffers harm.

Chapter 3

The Company You Keep

T'S A COLD MID-FEBRUARY DAY HERE in the cold and frozen north. The groundhog didn't see his shadow, thereby promising us an early spring. Of course, he lied ... again. Someday I'm going to shoot that oversized rodent and eat his liver for breakfast. I know that sounds harsh, but I just don't like people or animals messing with my early spring.

I'm sitting in my Honda Pilot in the middle of my hometown cemetery, writing and thinking, cogitating on the complexities of the universe, ruminating on all things I don't understand, and coming up blank and confused more often than not. There's just so much about life that I still don't understand.

I was watching *Winnie the Pooh* with my kids a few months back, and was confounded by the wisdom of the simple. Pooh Bear was talking to Christopher Robin, but was having trouble deciphering what the human was saying to him. Pooh

Bear, being a very polite personality, apologized for his lack of intellectual prowess by saying:

> *"For I am a bear of very little brain, and*
> *long words bother me."*

> — *a.a. milne*

It's probably not a good sign that I identify with a stuffed animal, even though he does come to life from time to time. However, for a bear of very little brain, Pooh strikes me as possessing a rather simple, but sensible brand of wildlife wisdom. Pooh Bear doesn't know a lot about the world beyond the hundred-acre woods, but what he does know, he knows very well, because he experiences it at a visceral level and with the faith and simplicity of a child.

> When you let crazy people into your life, then your life gets crazy.

I too am a bear of very little brain. But it doesn't take a rocket scientist to figure out that if you hang around with the wrong crowd, you're going to get yourself into trouble. Most of us learned that while still in elementary school. But have you noticed that some people, no matter how old they get, or how much heartache visits them, they never seem to learn that simple lesson? It's really quite amazing when you think about it.

Long ago I learned this very simple maxim: "When you let crazy people into your life, then your life gets crazy."

A few months back someone told me that 80 percent of all murder victims are killed by someone they know. I found that hard to believe, so I did my own research. Here's what I found out.

Homicide is defined by the FBI as "the willful (non-negligent) killing of one human being by another,"

According to the 2017 FBI Uniform Crime Report, a total of 15,129 murders were tracked in the study. Of those 15,129 murders, 6,103 victims knew their attacker - most of them were killed by relatives. That lends credence to the old saying "familiarity breeds contempt." Or, the better you know someone, the more likely you are to kill them. I found that rather sad, since the people who should be loving you the most are members of your own family. I thought that might be unique to America, but then discovered that in South Africa 80 percent of their victims are also being killed by people they know.

> Over 80 percent of all murder victims knew their attacker.

Of those 15,129 victims in the FBI UCR only 1,469 were known to have been killed by strangers. Another disturbing fact was that 7,557 of the murders went unsolved. That's almost exactly 50 percent. So, when you do the math, for just the murders where the relationship is known, it goes like this:

6103 - knew attacker

1469 - were killed by strangers

7572 - total murders

19.4% - killed by strangers

80.6% - killed by someone they know

I was amazed.

Those numbers really made me reconsider who I hung out with. Chances are, you already know the person who is going to kill you. My mom always told me never to hang out with the wrong crowd, but, I figured "Hey, you're just my mom! What do you know?" How would she know anything? It's not like she's in the FBI.

> *Experts and police agree you are more*
> *likely to be killed by your spouse, a relative,*
> *acquaintance, employee or business partner*
> *than by a stranger in a random act of crime.*
> *In fact 80 percent more likely as revealed in*
> *an analysis of 2 000 murders by the Institute*
> *of Security Studies and the police.*

So, how do you know who is the wrong crowd? The Bible gives us some pretty good clues.

Wrong Crowd Examples

> *Do not make friends with a hot-tempered*
> *person, do not associate with one easily*
> *angered,*

> *Proverbs 22:24 (NIV)*

> *But now I am writing to you that you must*
> *not associate with anyone who claims to be*
> *a brother or sister but is sexually immoral*
> *or greedy, an idolater or slanderer, a*
> *drunkard or swindler. Do not even eat with*
> *such people.*

> *1 Corinthians 5:11 (NIV)*

Wow! Those are some really heavy hitters! Don't make friends with people who get angry. That makes sense. You've certainly heard the phrase "crimes of passion." In the FBI crime report I noticed that two thirds of the murders were committed with firearms, except when a spouse, boyfriend/girlfriend or close relative was the murderer. In those cases, the weapon of choice was bare hands, blunt objects and knives.

When people fly into a rage, they do things they wouldn't normally do. They seem to lose temporary control, and they make it personal. And because these murders are so passionate, they tend to be extremely sudden and extremely violent.

The Bible also warns against people who are sexually immoral. Examples could be people who have sex with lots of partners, and people who cheat on their spouse. These acts show lack of loyalty and self-control, as well as a preoccupation with selfishness and lusts of the flesh. People who are sexually immoral cannot be trusted and shouldn't be associated with.

> You can pick your friends - but you're stuck with your relatives!

Have you ever heard the phrase "You can pick your friends, but you're stuck with your relatives." That's a tough one, because all of us have at least one crazy relative who is greedy, immoral, angry, filled with rage and sometimes even hatred. You can't change these people, but you can choose to limit your contact with them, and be on your guard when they're around you and your family.

The relative might even be your wife or husband. This was the case in my second marriage. My wife had multiple affairs, and, after being caught the second time, didn't even try to hide the arrangement. That was a very emotional time for me. I never wanted to kill either one of them, but, I do remember getting angry a time or two.

And what about people with drinking and drug-related

problems? My second wife was also an alcoholic. Any type of addiction is a wild card. The addiction becomes so powerful that it trumps any love they may feel for family members. This can become very frustrating and painful for the spouse who wants to save the marriage.

> **Domestic violence usually involves drugs, alcohol, mental illness and infidelity.**

Ask any cop about drugs and alcohol. Most crimes, especially those domestically related, are associated with drugs, alcohol and infidelity. Most cops refer to alcohol as "stupid juice." People don't get smarter after drinking to excess; they get dumber and dumber, meaner, and lose their inhibitions. That's why God says to stay away from these people. They will hurt you and drag you down.

When someone is under the influence of drugs and alcohol; they are temporarily insane. It's like rage in that regard, because people will do and say things they normally would not.

I think most of us realize we shouldn't let bad people into our lives, but ... we all seem to replace wisdom with hope. Hope that they'll change. Hope that the loved one will be different, that their love will conquer their deceit, or addiction or rage or malice. But this is seldom the case. Once a person gives themselves over to sin, they should not be associated with.

> *Having lost all sensitivity, they have given themselves over to sensuality so as to indulge in every kind of impurity, and they are full of greed.*

Ephesians 4:19 (NIV)

But now you might be asking: Who are the right kind of people?

Right Crowd Examples

> *But the fruit of the Spirit is love, joy,*
> *peace, forbearance, kindness, goodness,*
> *faithfulness, gentleness and self-control.*
> *Against such things there is no law.*

Galatians 5:22-23 (NIV)

I always liked that verse, but found it impossible to attain on my own strength. But hey! We're marksmen, so let's shoot for the bullseye!

> *"A man is known by the company he keeps"*

— Aesop

People know us by our fruits. But they also know us by the company we keep, so keep good company.

> *Do not be misled: Bad company corrupts*
> *good character.*

1 Corinthians 15:33 (NIV)

When you place a rotten apple on top of a bushel of healthy and beautiful fruit, what will happen. It's predictable. All the fruit will rot. Stay away from the bad apples. Look for spirit-filled people who are positive, God-fearing and who seek after a relationship with God. Those are the ones who hold you accountable; friends to last a lifetime, and will help you make it through life with the least amount of pain and suffering. And, as an added bonus ... they won't murder you in your sleep!

Things to Remember

1. You probably already know your killer.

2. Living a virtuous life adds to your own longevity.

3. Don't let crazy people into your life.

4. Choose friends who make your family more secure.

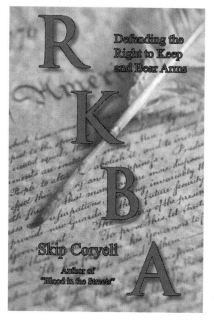

Columbine and Virginia Tech were not good omens. The victims there were unarmed sheep, who hid beneath desks and chairs, simply cowering as they died. They said "Baa" as they were being slaughtered. Something basic to our society has to change. It's time to stand and fight while we still can. And if our politicians tell us we can't protect our children in a daycare center, a post office, or a church, then we show them the door. We vote them out. We recall them. We take out the trash! That's the attitude that America was founded on. Somewhere along the timeline, America has lost it's way, we've lost our instinct for survival; it's no longer "fight or flight"; it's just plain "cower and die"!

Don't cower in the face of crime! Read this book and make your stand. That's one of the themes in Skip Coryell's new book *RKBA: Defending the Right to Keep and Bear Arms*.

II Samuel 11:14-16 (NIV)

14 In the morning David wrote a letter to Joab and sent it with Uriah. 15 In it he wrote, "Put Uriah out in front where the fighting is fiercest. Then withdraw from him so he will be struck down and die."

16 So while Joab had the city under siege, he put Uriah at a place where he knew the strongest defenders were. 17 When the men of the city came out and fought against Joab, some of the men in David's army fell; moreover, Uriah the Hittite died.

> *criminal* [krim-uh-nl] noun
> a person guilty or convicted of a crime.

Chapter 4

Criminal Actors

and King David

I THINK THE RECORD IS QUITE CLEAR that King David was a criminal. In law enforcement we would refer to him as a Violent Criminal Actor (VCA). Now, I understand that very few sermons will refer to King David, a man after God's own heart, as a violent criminal. However, if you look at his acts and the definition of the word *criminal*, then you can't deny it. King David was a criminal.

Why do I say this? Let me put it to you this way.

Check out this excerpt from the New York Post.

> *Denise Williams, 48, was convicted Friday in the death of her high school sweetheart, Mike Williams, who disappeared in December 2000 while on a hunting trip to*

Lake Seminole in Florida. She faced charges of first-degree murder, conspiracy and accessory after the fact.

The jury deliberated for around eight hours before finding Denise guilty of all charges. The murder charge comes with a mandatory sentence of life in prison.

Prosecutors argued Denise was having an affair with Mike's best friend, Brian Winchester, before his death. They alleged the lovers plotted to kill him so they could be together and she could cash in on his $1.75 million life insurance policy.

Our culture is no stranger to this type of story and we have a name for it: Love Triangle Murder Plot.

King David saw Bathsheba and he wanted her, so he sent for her and slept with her. David made her pregnant, so, in an effort to hide his tracks, David had one of his underlings send the innocent husband, Uriah, to his certain death on the battlefield.

> King David saw Bathsheba and he wanted her, so he sent for her and slept with her.

What is the difference between King David and Denise Williams? They both committed murder. They both are guilty as charged.

But David never went to prison, because he was the king. That doesn't sound fair. In fact, he went on to marry Bathsheba. So he killed the husband and took his wife as his own. It looked to David as if he'd just gotten away with murder. However, God is not to be trifled with.

God saw David's crime and sent the prophet, Nathan, who put it like this to the king.

> *1 The Lord sent Nathan to David. When he came to him, he said, "There were two men in a certain town, one rich and the other poor. 2 The rich man had a very large number of sheep and cattle, 3 but the poor man had nothing except one little ewe lamb he had bought. He raised it, and it grew up with him and his children. It shared his food, drank from his cup and even slept in his arms. It was like a daughter to him.*

> *4 "Now a traveler came to the rich man, but the rich man refrained from taking one of his own sheep or cattle to prepare a meal for the traveler who had come to him. Instead, he took the ewe lamb that belonged to the poor man and prepared it for the one who had come to him."*

> *5 David burned with anger against the man and said to Nathan, "As surely as the Lord lives, the man who did this must die! 6 He must pay for that lamb four times over, because he did such a thing and had no pity."*

> *7 Then Nathan said to David, "You are the man! This is what the Lord, the God of Israel, says: 'I anointed you king over Israel, and I delivered you from the hand of Saul.*

> *II Samuel 12:1-7 (NIV)*

Be sure your sins will find you out. I'm so glad that God held David accountable for his crime. It is good when our friends show us the error of our ways.

So let's get back to my original question. What's the difference between King David and Denise Williams? They are both murderers. Here's the difference. When confronted with his crime, King David responded in anguish and repentance:

> *13 Then David said to Nathan, "I have sinned against the Lord."*
>
> *II Samuel 12:8 (NIV)*

David wept and repented of his sin. He fell down on his face and he fasted and prayed to God asking for forgiveness. Was he still a murderer? Sure, after all Uriah was still dead. That's not something you can take back with any amount of repentance and humility.

> **Evil exists. Some day evil will visit your door. Will you be ready?**

So, why am I telling you this story? Because I want you to understand the nature of the evil that you and your family will be facing every time you leave your home, sometimes even inside your home. Because evil may visit your door; it may even live inside your home from time to time.

King David was a man after God's own heart, despite the fact that he was a murderer. He screwed up big time, but he also responded in the proper manner. Evil doesn't do that. Evil laughs in the face of justice, in the face of suffering and accountability. Here's a case in point via the Associated Press:

SACRAMENTO, Calif. (AP) — The suspect being tried in the slayings of two Northern California sheriff's deputies called one slain officer's partner a "coward" and repeatedly and profanely interrupted the start of his murder trial Tuesday.

Prosecutor Rod Norgaard was describing in his opening statement how Deputy Scott Brown retreated under heavy fire that killed his partner, Sacramento sheriff's Deputy Danny Oliver, outside a Sacramento motel in October 2014.

Luis Enrique Monroy Bracamontes grinned, then called Brown a "coward" before he was warned by Sacramento Superior Court Judge Steve White to remain silent, The Sacramento Bee reported.

"I wish I had killed more of the mother———," Bracamontes told jurors, adding that "I will break out soon and I will kill more, kill whoever gets in front of me… There's no need for a f—— trial."

I think most of us don't understand the true face of evil, how violent it can be, how callus, how cold and how calculating.

> **psychopath** [sahy-kuh-path] noun
> 1. a person with a psychopathic personality, which manifests as amoral and antisocial behavior, lack of ability to love or establish meaningful personal relationships, extreme egocentricity, failure to learn from experience, etc.

Real evil doesn't feel bad for its actions. It laughs at them and mocks the judge. Evil craves blood. Evil self-gratifies, and is eager to kill or destroy anything or anyone that gets in the way of its own pleasure and advancement. *The thief comes but to kill, steal and destroy.*

Fortunately, there are very few true psychopaths in this world. However, the number appears to grow as our society continues to step away from God and his rules and accountability. I encourage you today to step closer to God, to repent of any sin in your life and to steer your family on a True North moral compass heading in life.

> How could a murderer be a man after God's own heart?

There have been times in my life when I did stupid things, mean things, even committed terrible acts. There were times when I hurt people both physically and emotionally. But I always came back to God. I always repented. I always felt bad about my crimes, fell down on my face and cried out to God for forgiveness.

King David was a murderer, but that single act of his was an exception to the rule; it was not his defining characteristic. In general, through most of his life, David was filled with humility, courage, compassion and a desire to do right and to please the Lord.

So, in conclusion, King David was, without a doubt, a murderer. However, he was not evil. In the end, in the final analysis, judging David by the totality of his circumstances and the whole of his life, he really was a man after God's own heart ... most of the time.

The Life of David

1035 BC - David is born in the town of Bethlehem.

1025 BC - Samuel anoints the shepherd David as the future king of Israel.

1023 BC - David serves as a minstrel in Saul's court.

1020 BC - David kills Goliath.

1010 BC - King Saul makes David a commander in his army.

1008 BC - King Saul tries to kill David.

1005 BC   David spares Saul's life.

1000 BC - The Amalekites are destroyed by David and his men.

993 BC - David is anointed king of Judah.

992 BC   David plans to build a temple for God. – 2 Samuel 7

980 BC - David sleeps with Bathsheba and has her husband killed.

976 BC - David's son, Absalom, revolts.

974 BC - Absalom killed by Joab.

963 BC - Adonijah, David's fourth son revolts against David. Solomon is crowned king

961 BC - David dies. Solomon becomes king of Israel.

Natalie Katrell was a single mother. Her daughter, six-year old Amethyst, seemed like a miniature copy of herself, with long, blonde hair, shining blue eyes, and a smile that softened the hearts of most people who looked upon her. But neither Natalie nor Amethyst could see the man watching them. He always stayed off in the shadows, hidden around corners, or gazing from behind the innocent pages of a paperback book. Sometimes he sipped tea while at other times he nursed a vanilla latte with a double shot of espresso. But always, without fail, he watched Natalie and her daughter. He was obsessed and Natalie was his next chosen one. What would you do if a serial killer began stalking you and your child? Natalie Katrell was not a violent woman, but when the serial killer pushed, she pushed back! With the help of Sam Colton, NRA personal protection instructor, Natalie got armed and dangerous!

Genesis 4:9 (NIV)

Then the Lord said to Cain, "Where is your brother Abel?" "I don't know," he replied. "Am I my brother's keeper?"

Chapter 5

My Brother's Keeper

MANY PEOPLE IN THE CONCEALED carry industry spend a lot of time discussing, and, even teaching, that if you carry a gun for personal defense, that you should routinely mind your own business. And by that I mean, if you see someone being mugged or raped or murdered, these people espouse that you should simply call nine-one-one and then hang back and be a good witness for the police. They say this because it will keep you out of legal trouble. Sometimes this is the right response, but sometimes ... it is not.

I always tell my students that all of self-defense is scenario-based and there are an infinite number of scenarios. So, when someone tells me I should never get involved in other people's business, then ... well, I balk at their generalization. I think there's a balance point for everyone, and that balance point changes, depending on your abilities.

For example, I was teaching a concealed carry class a few years back, and I asked my students what they would do if they were in a gas station, back by the pop cooler, when a man walked in with a pistol and was robbing the store. I always get a myriad of answers when I ask this, and I think that's appropriate.

I asked one lady, about age sixty, and she told me she would open up the pop cooler, climb inside to hide and wait for the police to come. Everyone in the class laughed, but when we got out on the range and saw how bad a shot she was, we realized that her decision had been wise.

> Not everyone has the ability to intervene in the affairs of others.

Not everyone has the ability to successfully intervene in other people's affairs, especially affairs concerning deadly force. Let's face it, gunfighting is a skillset, and it doesn't just happen. You have to learn and then practice, or you just might die in a puddle of your own blood, puke and urine.

Not everyone should intervene ... but some of us should.

YouTube can be a great training tool, and I visit it often to watch videos that help me in my training. One day I was watching a video out of South America. An old man, about seventy-plus years old was sitting on the sidewalk with a pit-bull attached to his wrist. The dog's teeth were biting in, and the man was slowly bleeding to death. A crowd of people surrounded him to watch and to video the event. The video lasted over five minutes, but no one helped the man.

The old man died right there on the sidewalk while witnesses looked on. I was appalled.

Why hadn't any of them intervened? Why didn't they pick up a board and club the dog on the head? The police arrived 15 minutes later, but it was too late.

I would not have hesitated to kill that animal. To me, it was a cut-and-dried issue. The dog was killing the man. He needed help. Solution: Kill the dog.

It's easy to say, "Well, that was in South America, Skip. That kind of thing doesn't happen in America?" Really? I beg to differ with you. It happens all the time here as well. Check out this excerpt from the Chicago Tribune.

> *The woman was pinned to the ground by her attacker, who straddled her. She was screaming when the door of the train car opened at the North and Clybourn stop.*
>
> *Another man boarded the car. She screamed for help, hoping the man would do something. But, she told police, the man took off.*
>
> *Police said no calls about the attack came in from North and Clybourn around the time of the attack. The man I call the Bad Samaritan apparently did nothing to try to help.*
>
> *And now she holds him in greater contempt than the attacker.*
>
> *"Honestly I feel like I was mad at the guy who tried to rape me, but to be perfectly honest, I was more mad at the guy who didn't help me," said the young woman.*

*"Because he didn't stop the crime, he could
have helped me, but he just didn't want to, so
I feel like ..." she paused. "He was worse."*

It was easy to find the above story. I just did an online search on the string "woman attacked, screamed, no one helps." The search string revealed over 129 million results.

America ... how far have we fallen?

Since when is walking away from a woman being raped considered to be sound, acceptable and wise behavior? That's a good question, and I don't know the exact answer to that. However, I do know that Americans were not always this way. Sure, a certain amount of cowards and selfish people have always been with us, but ... they were not the norm in the America I grew up in. Today? I think maybe they are.

I understand fear ... believe me I do, and, lest you think of me as holier than thou and self-righteous, let me recount an embarrassing and shameful story from my youth.

I was at a basketball game at my home school. My friend and I were in the bathroom, when two older boys walked in. They were strangers, and we felt intimidated by their presence and the way they were looking at us. I believe my friend and I were about 13 years old at the time. My friend was taller and stronger than I. I weighed about 90 pounds soaking wet. I was short and weak, and not yet into puberty. I could tell that these two bigger and stronger boys were trouble, so I tried to leave. They blocked my path. My friend tried to leave too, but was also blocked.

> I was short
> and weak
> and weighed
> 90 pounds
> soaking wet.

The leader of the two walked up to my friend and announced that he was going to fight him. Of course, my friend tried to talk his way out of it, but the older, stronger aggressor would have no part of it. The aggressor told me to wait outside with his friend until he was done. I hesitated, not knowing what to do. I was terrified as the other boy grabbed me by the arm and escorted me to the door. Outside the bathroom, the older boy looked me in the eye and said, "Don't move. Don't say anything. Just wait."

I complied.

That one act of compliance, that moment when I gave in to my fear and allowed my friend to get beat up, has haunted me for almost fifty years now. There was no excuse for what I did, and I am deeply grieved and ashamed of my actions. But I can't take them back.

> From that moment on, I vowed that I would never again leave a friend in need.

About thirty seconds later, the aggressor rushed out of the bathroom and ran off into the crowded school. I ran into the bathroom to check on my friend. He was wiping the blood off his lip, but otherwise okay. Now, it would have been easy for me to justify my actions. After all, I was a head shorter than them and about forty pounds too light to take them on and win.

But ... a funny thing happened on the way to adulthood. The guilt and shame of my actions overcame me, and I vowed that I would never again leave a friend in need. I started doing push-ups. I lifted weights. I learned how to fight.

I didn't like the person I'd become. After all, with friends like me ... who needs enemies? So I changed. Later on I joined the Marine Corps and I changed even more.

When I sat down this morning to write this chapter, I wasn't thinking about those shameful events from my childhood. In fact, this is the first time in my life that I've ever admitted to those events.

> You don't have to remain weak. You don't have to remain a victim.

If I'm honest with myself, even if I'd chosen to fight alongside my friend, I would have been little help to him. I didn't know how to fight, and I was just a skinny, little runt of a kid. Nonetheless, I could have done something. I could have screamed as loud as I could for help. I could have tried to scratch the boy's eyes out. Instead, I complied. I gave into my fear. I don't like that, and it will never happen again.

Truth is, I was just a boy back then, and I need to forgive myself and move on. I've done that. But forgiveness doesn't change the past. But that one event did change my future.

In my experience, 10 percent of life is comprised of the events that happen to you, but 90 percent of life is how you respond to that 10 percent.

When I think back to the woman from my concealed carry class who said she would have climbed into the cooler and waited for the police, I can't help but sympathize with her. Because I understand cowardice. I understand shame and fear. I understand the feeling of victimhood.

Now, I understand that some of you think that I'm being unreasonable, asking that an elderly woman stand up and help protect a stranger in need. But I don't think so. The 13-year-old version of me, was not capable of protecting myself, let alone my friend or a stranger. However, that didn't absolve me of my responsibility.

Weak people don't have to stay weak.

Cowards can become brave.

It is a documented fact that a 70-year-old woman with training and a gun can realistically prevail over an armed thug. Remember that and hold yourself accountable. Don't fall into the social trend of fashionable and pseudo-wise cowardice.

Cane was being a smart-alek when he asked God "Am I my brother's keeper?" After all, think about it. Do you really want to emulate Cane, the first murderer of recorded history?

Are you presently a bad shot? If so, then get trained and practice. Upgrade yourself. Are you weak in empty-handed fighting? Then train and change that. Why? Because whether you admit it or not, you really are your brother's keeper. All of us are. God has charged us to love one another. And then he said, "Greater love has no person than this, that he lay down his life for a friend."

We are all brothers and sisters in the Lord. Train and protect each other.

Things to Remember

1. Not everyone can or should intervene in all self-defense situations.

2. Everyone should continually upgrade their self-defense skills.

3. Self-defense is scenario-based, and all scenarios are extremely fluid and dynamic, changing from moment to moment.

4. Victims are born everyday. But to remain a victim is a personal choice. Choose strength. Choose training.

5. 10 percent of life is comprised of the events that happen to you, but 90 percent of life is how you respond to that 10 percent.

"Wow! Skip Coryell's new book Blood in the Streets is good stuff! It's killer! Read it and hammer on! Upgrade!"

-- Ted Nugent - Legendary hunter, Rock-n-roller and author of "God, Guns, and Rock-n-Roll"

This book is important to anyone who wants to better protect their families!

Deuteronomy 32:39 (NIV)

39 "See now that I myself am he! There is no god besides me. I put to death and I bring to life, I have wounded and I will heal, and no one can deliver out of my hand.

Chapter 6

Should Christians Kill?

FOR MANY DECADES I STRUGGLED with this question: should Christians kill? And, in the end, I decided that "Yes, there are indeed times in a Christian's life when they are morally justified in taking the life of another."

I studied the Bible, and then bumped it up against the test of real life and my own experiences, but I took it even a step further: not only is it sometimes moral to kill, but there are also times when it is immoral to not kill.

In my book *Civilian Combat*, I explain that all of self-defense is scenario-based, and all scenarios are extremely fluid and dynamic, meaning that they change from moment to moment and are very susceptible to outside influence. Here's what that means to me: we should take into consideration the context of the killing.

I recall decades ago in college I was taking a philosophy and religion class, and the professor brought up the question of situational ethics. For our purposes we'll define situational ethics as: "looking past the right and wrong, and performing what the circumstances demand."

The classic example was this:

> *You live in Nazi-occupied Holland during*
> *World War II, and the SS beat on your door.*
> *You answer it, and they demand to know:*
> *Are you harboring any Jews in your house?*
> *You know full well that if you say "yes,"*
> *then the Jews will die. But if you say "no"*
> *they will live.*

This is a real-life example that happened many times during that war. The Bible says "Do not bear false witness." That means do not lie.

> *Question: is it moral to tell the truth,*
> *thereby condemning people to torture and*
> *death? Or, is it moral to lie and save their*
> *lives?*

That has always been a tough question for me. Here's what I determined in my own life: morality does not kill innocent people. To the contrary ... morality protects innocent people.

The criminal justice system determines legality by invoking something called the totality of the circumstances. Here it is in a nutshell:

> *"At the time you acted, you must have*
> *honestly and reasonably believed that you*
> *were in danger of being killed or seriously*
> *injured."*

On earth, we will be judged by a jury of our peers, but, in the after life, we will be judged by the great Almighty Creator of the Universe. That seems like a big difference to me. Men are fallible. They make mistakes. It's true. There are a few innocent men in prison. Think about it. Have you ever read *Foxe's Book of Martyrs*? I tried a few times, but I just couldn't stomach the brutality of how these people were tortured and killed. Many of them were tried and found guilty, then condemned to death. But they were all innocent.

God is the one, true judge, the perfect judge. He will determine the fate of the living and the dead, and He will do it not based on man's law, but on God's law and the condition of their heart.

> *"I the LORD search the heart and examine the mind, to reward each person according to their conduct, according to what their deeds deserve."*

> *Jeremiah 17:10 (NIV)*

I believe that God will judge our actions based on the "totality of the circumstances." God searches our hearts and minds to determine the intent of our heart. I think He's smart enough to do that.

> *"The Lord does not look at the things man looks at. Man looks at the outward appearance, but the Lord looks at the heart."*

> *1 Samuel 16:7 (NIV)*

It's obvious to me that God looks on the heart of man, that He knows our every thought, emotion and intent. God judges our hearts. He knows our heart. But here's a question that few people ask: "Do you know your own heart?" Always listen to your thoughts. Judge them, test them, try them.

I believe that God will indeed judge based on the totality of the circumstances. And, if that's true, then shouldn't we also give God the benefit of the doubt and judge him on the same basis. (Yes, I understand that we aren't capable of judging God, but, many people, like I did when young, try in vain to do it nonetheless.)

Here's what I mean by that: it's not enough to look at God's actions, but you should go one step further and ask the question: why did God do that?

Many people struggle with the fact that God, throughout the old testament, commanded Moses, Joshua, King David, just to name a few, to destroy entire communities.

> *16 However, in the cities of the nations*
> *the Lord your God is giving you as an*
> *inheritance, do not leave alive anything that*
> *breathes. 17 Completely destroy them—the*
> *Hittites, Amorites, Canaanites, Perizzites,*
> *Hivites and Jebusites—as the Lord your God*
> *has commanded you.*
>
> *Deuteronomy 20:16,17 (NIV)*

I think it's important to understand God's reasons for ordering the death of so many people. Read the next verse in that passage.

> *18 Otherwise, they will teach you to*
> *follow all the detestable things they do in*
> *worshiping their gods, and you will sin*
> *against the Lord your God.*
>
> *Deuteronomy 20:18 (NIV)*

God sends people into battle for a positive purpose, never for the simple sake of destruction and death. There is always a positive qualifier to fall back on. God understands the nature of evil. He knows that, if allowed unchecked, evil will run its course and all humanity will be corrupted. All of human history has proven God correct. God is a surgeon, and He cuts out the cancer before it can kill the entire soul of humanity.

God doesn't view death the same way that you and I do. Probably because he's infinite and immortal, or perhaps because He's spiritual. God puts greater emphasis on the spiritual realm than He does the physical realm. After all, physical things are temporary, whether we're talking about your physical body or your possessions, but the spirit lives on forever. This is evidenced by the words of Jesus.

> *19 "Do not store up for yourselves treasures on earth, where moths and vermin destroy, and where thieves break in and steal. 20 But store up for yourselves treasures in heaven, where moths and vermin do not destroy, and where thieves do not break in and steal. 21 For where your treasure is, there your heart will be also.*
>
> *Matthew 6:19-21 (NIV)*

> *"You have heard that it was said, 'You shall not commit adultery. 28 But I tell you that anyone who looks at a woman lustfully has already committed adultery with her in his heart. 29 If your right eye causes you to stumble, gouge it out and throw it away. It is better for you to lose one part of your body than for your whole body to be thrown into hell. 30 And if your right hand causes you*

to stumble, cut it off and throw it away. It is
better for you to lose one part of your body
than for your whole body to go into hell.

Matthew 5:28-30 (NIV)

God does not kill lightly. In fact, He would prefer to create, than to kill. If you doubt that, lift up your head and look around you. God's entire creation is beautiful and awesome, and nothing is created that was not spoken into existence by God.

One of my favorite movies is *Gettysburg*, with Martin Sheen as Robert E. Lee and Tom Beringer as General Longstreet. On the eve of battle, General Lee makes this statement to General Longstreet:

"To be a good soldier, you must love the
army. To be a good commander, you must be
willing to order the death of the thing you
love."

I think God must be like that, at least in this respect. He loves His creation so much, that He sent His son to die for it, but, at the same time, He was also willing to kill His creation in order to save it. We see that play out over and over throughout the Bible.

God destroyed most of His creation, all but Noah, his wife and sons and their wives.

21 Every living thing that moved on land
perished—birds, livestock, wild animals, all
the creatures that swarm over the earth, and
all mankind. 22 Everything on dry land that
had the breath of life in its nostrils died. 23
Every living thing on the face of the earth
was wiped out; people and animals and the

creatures that move along the ground and
the birds were wiped from the earth. Only
Noah was left, and those with him in the ark.

Genesis 5:21-23 (NIV)

God rained down fire and brimstone on the cities of Sodom and Gomorrah, destroying every last man, woman and child still inside.

24 Then the Lord rained down burning
sulfur on Sodom and Gomorrah—from
the Lord out of the heavens. 25 Thus he
overthrew those cities and the entire plain,
destroying all those living in the cities—and
also the vegetation in the land.

Genesis 19:24-25 (NIV)

There was a time in my life when I struggled with the concept of God killing those He created. It was between my first and second marriages, at a time when I was at my lowest, my deepest and my darkest. It was my own personal "dark night of the soul." I came to the point where I doubted God's goodness and His love for me. There was nothing but despair in the wake of that ship.

But ... how can one reconcile this:

16 For God so loved the world that he gave
his one and only Son, that whoever believes
in him shall not perish but have eternal life.

John 3:16 (NIV)

With this?

40 So Joshua subdued the whole region,
including the hill country, the Negev, the
western foothills and the mountain slopes,

> *together with all their kings. He left no*
> *survivors. He totally destroyed all who*
> *breathed, just as the Lord, the God of Israel,*
> *had commanded.*

> *Joshua 10:40 (NIV)*

In my youth, I knew more than God. But, as I aged, I began to wonder ... Is it remotely possible that God is:

- smarter than us?
- more complicated than us?
- more complete than us?

After many years of pain and rumination, I answered my own questions with a resounding "yes!"

I have come to believe that God sees physical death in a different light than us mortals. He sees death more completely, in a macro-cosmic view, from the outside looking in.

God sees physical death as a rite of passage, as going from the physical realm into the spiritual realm. The physical life that you and I lead is simply the starting point, the proving grounds, the test that we take and pass before entering into the next state of existence, which is spiritual.

Why does God kill? God kills evil to protect the innocent. And that is exactly why you and I are also morally justified in killing evil, under certain conditions.

This is by far the biggest struggle that Christians who carry a gun have to go through.

Should Christians kill?

The answer is a qualified "yes."

- When a man is beating your wife with a baseball bat, then yes, you can kill.
- When a mass shooter walks into McDonald's Playland and starts executing children, then yes,

you can kill.

- When a pedophile is in the process of kidnapping your child for his own perversion, then yes, you can kill.

Let me say it again. Not only are there times you "can" kill, but there are also times when you "must" kill. To withhold aid to the innocent is an immoral act. If you don't have a gun, then attack with your bare hands.

I look at our culture and see a flock of sheep who have been brainwashed into believing that any form of violence is bad. That's just not true. God is both violent and loving. We were made in His image, so therefore, humans are also violent and loving. We have the capacity to hurt or to heal, to wound or to kill.

Pure evil does not circle up, hold hands and gently sing *Kumbaya*. To the contrary. Jesus defined evil for us when he said:

> *10 The thief comes only to steal and kill and destroy; I have come that they may have life, and have it to the full.*
>
> *John 10:10 (NIV)*

You have God's permission, even His blessing. When the thief comes to kill, then you are morally availed the use of deadly force. Resist deadly evil.

While in the Marine Corps, I was trained as a radio operator. One of my jobs was to call in fire missions. It could be mortars, artillery or air and naval gunfire. The spotter would call out the coordinates, and then walk the misses closer to the target by adjusting forward or back or left and right. Once the rounds were on target, the proper radio command was "fire for effect."

And that command I give to you. Once you know your heart, that you are defending the innocent, then aim true and fire for effect.

> *"There are no creatures that walk the earth, not even those animals we have labelled cowards, which will not show courage when required to defend themselves."*
>
> — *Alexandre Dumas, The Vicomte de Bragelonne*

If masculinity is toxic, then Jack Ruger is the cultural equivalent of a raging bull on steroids. Born and raised in the cold and frozen northern paradise of Michigan's upper peninsula, Chief of Police Jack Ruger is sworn to protect and defend the citizens of Jackpine. So when escaped killer Bobby Lee Harper descends on the town, threatening to kill him and all he holds dear, it's a formal declaration of war, and only one man will survive.

Exodus 15:3 (NIV)

3 The Lord is a warrior; the Lord is
his name.

Chapter 7

The Warrior Creed

MANY PEOPLE IN TODAY'S Christian church are uncomfortable with the term "warrior." And that confuses me a bit, because God Himself is a warrior, a conquering hero, a brave, indomitable deity who never gives up and never gives in.

My twelve-year-old son, Cedar, was wearing a t-shirt today, and on the back of it, I read this quote:

> *"It's hard to beat a man who never gives up."*
>
> – *Babe Ruth*

One of the nice things about warriors is they're not inclined to surrender. And how could a true warrior go into battle thinking of the prospect of giving up? A warrior thinks not of surrender, but attack; not of retreat, but of advance. I can't find a single place in the Bible where God surrendered or encouraged a man of God to surrender to evil.

Of course, as Christians, we are to surrender our life and our will to God, but not in battle against the enemy. To the contrary, God has always encouraged his children to stand against evil, both in the spiritual and physical realms.

Let's talk about the spiritual realm first.

In his letter to the Ephesians Paul wrote:

> *10 Finally, be strong in the Lord and in his mighty power. 11 Put on the full armor of God, so that you can take your stand against the devil's schemes.*

> *Ephesians 6:10-11 (NIV)*

Spiritual warfare is a prominent theme in the New Testament, and Paul, as well as Jesus Christ speak of it several times. Who else but a warrior needs the tools of a warrior. Paul describes these spiritual warfare tools to us in Ephesians.

> *14 Stand firm then, with the belt of truth buckled around your waist, with the breastplate of righteousness in place, 15 and with your feet fitted with the readiness that comes from the gospel of peace. 16 In addition to all this, take up the shield of faith, with which you can extinguish all the flaming arrows of the evil one. 17 Take the helmet of salvation and the sword of the Spirit, which is the word of God.*

> *Ephesians 6:14-17 (NIV)*

Paul chooses to use the basic warrior tools of that day to describe how we should resist evil: the belt of Truth, the breastplate of righteousness, the sandals of peace, the shield of faith, the helmet of salvation and the sword of the spirit. Spiritual evil should be resisted using the tools of spiritual warfare.

Jesus Christ, the Son of God, used spiritual warfare tools when he battled against Satan as He neared the end of his fasting in the desert at the beginning of His earthly ministry.

> *1 Then Jesus was led by the Spirit into the wilderness to be tempted by the devil. 2 After fasting forty days and forty nights, He was hungry.*

> *3 The tempter came to Him and said, "If You are the Son of God, tell these stones to become bread."*

> *Matthew 4:1-3 (NIV)*

This was Satan's first attack in this battle. Satan tried to stab Jesus with the sword of the spirit. But Jesus fought back.

> *4 But Jesus answered, "It is written:*

> *'Man shall not live on bread alone, but on every word that comes from the mouth of God."*

So Satan attacked Jesus again.

> *5 Then the devil took Him to the holy city and set Him on the pinnacle of the temple. 6 "If You are the Son of God," he said, "throw Yourself down. For it is written:*

> *'He will command His angels concerning You, and they will lift You up in their hands,*

> *so that You will not strike Your foot against*
> *a stone."*
>
> *Matthew 4:5-6 (NIV)*

Jesus deftly and expertly parried the blow.

> *7 Jesus replied, "It is also written: 'Do not*
> *put the Lord your God to the test."*
>
> *Matthew 4:7 (NIV)*

Satan is getting desperate at this point, so he pulled out all the stops and played his only trump card.

> *8 Again, the devil took Him to a very high*
> *mountain and showed Him all the kingdoms*
> *of the world and their glory. 9 "All this I*
> *will give You," he said, "if You will fall*
> *down and worship me."*
>
> *Matthew 4:8-9 (NIV)*

Jesus blocked with His shield and then attacked with His sword.

> *10 "Away from Me, Satan!" Jesus declared.*
> *"For it is written: 'Worship the Lord your*
> *God and serve Him only."*
>
> *11 Then the devil left Him, and angels came*
> *and ministered to Him.*
>
> *Matthew 4:10-11 (NIV)*

Game. Set. Match!
Jesus 1. Satan 0.

Notice the extreme confidence of the true warrior. Jesus

just kicked Satan's metaphorical butt in a down-and-out spiritual brawl. Satan tried to use the sword of the spirit, which is the word of God against Jesus. But Jesus would have none of it. In the spiritual realm, confidence is another name for faith. Jesus used the shield of faith to block and nullify all of Satan's attacks. Satan was quoting from the Bible, the very words of God Himself. So, why did Satan fail?

Several reasons come to mind.

1. Jesus wielded the sword of the spirit, and He was a master swordsman. No one knows a sword better than the maker of that sword. Satan didn't know the mind of God, therefore, he could never use God's words effectively against Him.

2. Jesus held high the shield of faith. Jesus was highly practiced in spiritual warfare. His faith was stronger than any human, simply because He was God incarnate. Let's face it; it really wasn't a fair fight from the outset. Jesus, the God of the universe, the Creator of heaven and earth has been kicking Satan's butt since the dawn of time. And since God exists in the spiritual realm as well as the physical realm, He is outside time and space and looking in. Jesus, in human form, though tempted, was able to use the shield of faith to parry all Satan's attacks.

3. Jesus was protected by the breastplate of righteousness. Jesus, being God, was without sin and therefore righteous. In the words of famous, secular rapper, MC Hammer, Jesus said to Satan, "You can't touch

this." Satan never laid a glove on the warrior Christ. And then Jesus put the hammer down and said, "Get thee behind me, Satan."

4. Jesus wore the belt of Truth. Not only did Jesus know the Truth, but He also firmly believed in it. Satan knew the Truth, but refused to believe it, therefore the belt of Truth does nothing for him, and will always be an ineffective tool in his hands. The faith of Jesus was higher than that of Satan.

> *18 But someone will say, "You have faith and I have deeds." Show me your faith without deeds, and I will show you my faith by my deeds. 19 You believe that God is one. Good for you! Even the demons believe that—and shudder.*
>
> *James 2:18-19 (NIV)*

5. Jesus' feet were fitted with the gospel of peace. Jesus was a mighty warrior, but He was also a reluctant warrior. He didn't want to fight. Satan came to Him and called Him out. Jesus prefers peace, as should all of His children. However, to quote King Arthur in the movie *First Knight*:

> *"There's a peace only to be found on the other side of war. If that war should come I will fight it!"*

More than anything else, Jesus wants peace, but He knows the nature and power of evil, and He is willing to fight for peace. He knows that He must fight, that sin must be violently defeated, and that's why He fought for us in a paradoxical way. He died for us on the cross. It was the ultimate battle where He conquered sin and death. Jesus is a mighty warrior, but He doesn't fight for the sake of fighting. Fighting is not an end, it is a means to gain peace.

"A thorn defends the rose, harming only those who would steal the blossom."

- Chinese Proverb

And now let's talk about the physical realm. I believe that the physical and spiritual realms are inextricably linked. The spiritual plane is higher, it binds all reality together, like the carrier wave in telecommunications, where the FM or AM signal is attached to the carrier and is transported through space. The spiritual realm is the carrier and the physical plane is attached to it.

God is the carrier, but He can move back and forth from the spirit realm to the physical realm. Sometimes people are allowed to touch the spiritual plane, but most of the time we live in the physical world. Right now, for instance, I'm in a cafe, drinking a diet Pepsi and people are moving all around me. I don't see any spirits here. That reminds me of that 1999 movie with Bruce Willis called *The Sixth Sense*. The boy, played by Haley Joel Osment, could see and experience spirits everywhere he went. I'm really glad I can't do that. The physical realm is tough enough without throwing in ghosts.

But when I leave this cafe. I'll have to walk down a crowded sidewalk into a not-so-safe neighborhood. I may be mugged. I may be murdered. I may be accosted in a number of ways. But I won't be seeing any dead people unless they are rotting on the sidewalk, taking the room-temperature challenge. But again, that's the physical realm.

I live in the physical. I work here. I breathe here. I get sick here. I get married here. I die here.

A friend of mine teaches Krav Maga. His name is Craig Gray, and he has created a program called The PeaceWalker Project. As Christians, we are called to live in peace with our fellow man, but what happens when your fellow man rapes your daughter? What happens when your fellow man stabs you with a knife? Does God expect you to sit idly by and watch?

Jesus didn't do that. Sure, He allowed the Jews and Romans to kill Him, but that was more His idea than theirs. It was in accordance with God's plan from the foundations of the earth.`And what about this scripture, which is so often quoted by pacifists?

> 38 *"You have heard that it was said, 'Eye*
> *for eye, and tooth for tooth. 39 But I tell you,*
> *do not resist an evil person. If anyone slaps*
> *you on the right cheek, turn to them the*
> *other cheek also.*

> *Matthew 5:38-39 (NIV)*

Only when you place these words of Jesus in context, will you truly understand what He really means.

In the culture and time of Jesus, a strike on the right cheek with the back of the hand was understood to be an insult. It was also forbidden in that culture to touch anyone with your left hand, because the left hand was used to do things considered unclean (like wiping your buttocks.) So when Jesus said to turn the other cheek, he was getting the listener's attention, because that would be a supreme insult. The point is, Jesus wasn't talking so much about violence as He was about insulting another man's integrity.

Jesus was saying "Go ahead and let people insult you. It's not a big deal." And He was right. I teach the same thing in my concealed carry classes. I teach my students that when they start carrying a firearm for personal protection, they must become the most polite people on the planet. You no longer can get into arguments or altercations of any kind. If someone insults you, turn the other cheek and walk away. Because the ante is upped when you're wearing a gun. Verbal confrontations can escalate into physical fights, and then you might have to shoot someone. Or, they might take your gun and shoot you. Either scenario is unacceptable, so just walk away. That's what I mean when I tell my students that a firearm is a tool of last resort.

Jesus was the first and the ultimate peacewalker, but He was also the supreme warrior. He avoided confrontations, but when the fight came to Him, He did not shrink from it. Jesus stood up for what was right ... even unto His own death.

In my opinion, Jesus is calling us to be "reluctant" warriors. One of my favorite prose is *The Warrior Creed*, written by Robert Humphrey:

The Warrior Creed

Wherever I walk,

everyone is a little bit safer
because I am there.

Wherever I am,

anyone in need has a friend.

Whenever I return home,

everyone is happy I am there.

–Robert L. Humphrey–

What is a Christian warrior supposed to be like?

1. He should have self-control.

> *19 My dear brothers and sisters, take note of this: Everyone should be quick to listen, slow to speak and slow to become angry, "*
>
> *"James 1:19 (NIV)*

2. He should be strong.

> *14 In the temple courts he found people selling cattle, sheep and doves, and others sitting at tables exchanging money. 15 So he made a whip out of cords, and drove all from the temple courts, both sheep and cattle; he scattered the coins of the money changers and overturned their tables.*
>
> *John 2:14-15 (NIV)*

3. He should be humble.

> *5 In your relationships with one another, have the same mindset as Christ Jesus: 6 Who, being in very nature a God, did not consider equality with God something to be used to his own advantage; 7 rather, he made himself nothing by taking the very nature b of a servant, being made in human likeness. 8 And being found in appearance as a man, he humbled himself by becoming obedient to death–even death on a cross.*
>
> *Philippians 2:5-8 (NIV)*

4. He is willing to die for others.

> *Greater love has no one than this: to lay*
> *down one's life for one's friends.*
>
> *John 15:13 (NIV)*

And to these traits he must add a great and studied skill in the arts of his trade. Don't settle for mediocrity. You are a protector and a defender, so you must hone your skills to a razor's edge. Other people will live or die based on your skill level, so always practice, always train.

Ask yourself this question: Do people feel safer when you walk into the room?

If not, then make a change.

Are you a friend to those in need?

If not, then make a change.

When you return home, are people happy with your presence?

If not, then make a change.

The ultimate protector and defender is Jesus Christ. Jesus is both lover and fighter. To become the best Christian warrior, you must also emulate Christ.

> *3 The Lord is a warrior; the Lord is his*
> *name.*
>
> *Exodus 15:3 (NIV)*

Things to Remember

1. The strong rarely surrender to the weak.

2. A true Christian warrior is willing to fight and die, if need be, to protect the innocent and the weak.

3. Where ever I walk, everyone should feel safer because I am there.

4. Jesus Christ is the ultimate peace walker. Strive to be like Christ.

5. Put on the whole armor of God to protect yourself both physically and spiritually.

6. With His voluntary death on the cross, Christ saved all of humanity. You can save the ones around you.

Psalm 144:1 (NIV)

Praise be to the Lord my Rock, who trains my hands for war, my fingers for battle.

Chapter 8

The Importance of Training

THE BIBLE TALKS A LOT ABOUT training, and not just training for battle, but about training and striving for excellence in every aspect of our lives. I think this one verse sums it up.

> *23 Whatever you do, work at it with all your heart, as working for the Lord, not for human masters, 24 since you know that you will receive an inheritance from the Lord as a reward.*

> *Colossians 3:23-24 (NIV)*

Of course, the full context is that Paul is talking to slaves, and is encouraging them to do their best, even in their unfortunate circumstances.

> *22 Slaves, obey your earthly masters in everything; and do it, not only when their eye is on you and to curry their favor, but*

> with sincerity of heart and reverence for the
> Lord.
>
> *Colossians 3:22 (NIV)*

But I think the point is clear, that the general concept of always doing your best, no matter what the circumstances, is still a valid one. God wants us to strive for excellence in every aspect of our lives.

> *31 So whether you eat or drink or whatever
> you do, do it all for the glory of God.*
>
> *1 Corinthians 10:31 (NIV)*

But does that include striving for excellence in the role as protector and defender? Let me put it another way ... why wouldn't it? Certainly there are limitations on 1 Corinthians 10:31. Common sense tells us there are just some things that one cannot do to the glory of God. The phrase "rape, pillage and plunder" comes to mind.

The role of protector and defender is a time-honored calling, one that has always been treasured and appreciated, especially by the weakest among us, those in the greatest need, like women and children.

> The role of protector and defender is a time-honored calling.

Speaking of women and children ... I'm getting a lot more females in my concealed carry classes. On the one hand, that's a very good thing, because women are more likely to be victims of violent crime than men. (According to FBI crime stats, women have a one in four chance of being victims of violent crime.) On the other hand, it's kind of sad.

Because women are taking classes and getting armed in order to protect themselves against the men who are supposed to be protecting them. A large portion of men in our society have absconded from their natural role.

abscond[ab-skond]

verb (used without object)
to depart in a sudden and secret manner, especially to avoid capture and legal prosecution:

When the natural protectors abandon ship, then others must take up the slack. Generally speaking, most women have less upper body strength, quickness and physical stamina than most men. So when a man becomes the aggressor rather than the defender, then women are forced to arm themselves for their own protection. I see that as a sad thing, because God created women with a natural nurturing superiority. They want to be nice, to be kind to others, and to raise children to do the same.

> A large portion of American men have forsaken their role as defenders and protectors.

Of course, a hard-corps feminist might take issue with that statement, but that's okay. In the absence of a male protector, the woman must fend for herself and her children. And single parents probably have the toughest job of all. I know, because I've been a custodial single-parent as well as a non-custodial single parent. It's tough enough raising kids in this world even when you have the support of a well-adjusted and loving spouse. I think single parenting must be like a lone warrior attacking a machine gun nest without benefit of fire support or reinforcements. It's a tough proposition. But then ... I digress.

Let's get back to training.

If you've already made the decision to carry a gun for personal and family defense ... well, then ... you might as well become good at it. I spent six years in the Marine Corps, and we did a lot of training. Quite frankly, it was peacetime, and there was nothing else to do. But the training is what makes a Marine different from other people. We weren't born different, we were taught to be different.

You should find that encouraging. Simply put, if I can become a Marine, based on training and proper mindset, then you can also become the protector and defender of the innocent, whether you are a man, a woman, a child, and regardless of your age and physical stature. Is it tougher for some than for others? Of course. But we do the best we can with what God gave us. God demands only that we strive for excellence. No more and no less.

> **Less than one percent of concealed carriers train beyond what is legally required.**

Here's the saddest part of all. Less than one percent of concealed carry holders ever go on to take any training beyond what is required by the government. This was determined by an exhaustive study done by Karl Rehn, an excellent trainer from Texas. If you'd like the details of Karl's study, just go to this URL:

http://blog.krtraining.com/beyond-the-one-percent-part-1/

What does that mean to me as a firearms and tactical trainer? First, it tells me a lot about human nature.

1. People are lazy, kind of like water that always follows the path of least resistance. (I've never seen water flow uphill, unless something really powerful is chasing it.) Running uphill is good for you, but few people do it.

2. People don't want to "be safe" they just want to "feel safe." First off, total safety is an illusion; it doesn't exist, but there are different levels of safety. And the more training you have, the safer you are. Most people don't really believe that anything bad will ever happen to them, and people will usually act on their beliefs. If you truly believed in your heart and soul that you'd one day be a victim of violent crime, then you'd do something about it. But most people are content to simply play the numbers. Odds are it will be someone else who gets mugged - not me. And for the most part that's true. You are safe. Until ... someone mugs you, kills you, rapes you, robs you, etc., etc., so on and so forth. So people relax and continue watching people getting mugged, robbed, raped and killed on their favorite television shows. It's much more comfortable that way. The way of the warrior is an uphill battle and not for the faint of heart.

> **Total safety is an illusion, but there are levels of safety you achieve through training.**

Feeling safe is easy. Take a short, government-mandated concealed carry class, apply for the permit, buy a gun, and then, "poof" like magic you are safe. The mere presence of your gun and concealed carry permit will ward off violence of any kind.

I think not.

Owning a gun doesn't make you a gun fighter any more than owning a guitar makes you a rock star.

You have to train.

Second, it tells me that over 99 percent of the time, I get only one shot at training you. When I look out at the room full of students, I know that I'll never see you again after today. You'll take the class, buy the gun, get the permit and then the gun will rust in your safe or a desk drawer.

One day you'll need the gun. Several things may happen:

1. You won't have the gun on you, because you never really believed in your heart that you'd ever need it. You will be a victim, and survive only at the good graces of the evil man holding a knife to your throat. Good luck with that.

2. You'll have the gun on you, but won't be able to survive the gun fight. Why? Because you lack the training. Gunfighting is a skill set composed of drawing, moving and shooting. You didn't learn that in your state-mandated one-day class. Because you lack the skills, you will die in a puddle of your own blood, puke and urine.

3. You have a heart attack. The adrenaline dump into your bloodstream will be too large a strain on your overweight and out-of-shape carcass you call a body. You will collapse to the ground, clutching at your chest, relishing the memory of a lifetime of processed sugar and saturated fats, as reruns of your favorite sitcoms flash before your eyes.

The immortal words of Lionel Barrymore come to mind:

> *"Do I paint a correct picture, or do I exaggerate?"*
>
> *–Henry F. Potter, It's a Wonderful Life*

Here's the bottom line: without proper, sharply-honed skills, you are not a complete warrior. You might think you are ... but you are not.

So many of us have this delusion that at the moment of truth, we will rise to a level beyond our training. You will step into the phone booth (if you can find one) don your leotards and cape and step out as Superman, ready to vanquish all foes, defeat any evil, and protect and defend the innocent.

But here's the real truth:

You are likely to fail. You are not prepared for battle. You will not rise to a level beyond your training in that moment of terror and angst. You will sink to a level below your training. That's the way it really happens. That's why the military trains over and over and over again. I recall being in the Marines, and being forced to disassemble my M16 over and over and over again. And they never told us why we were doing it. But later on I figured it out. The Marine Corps needed me to be able to operate my weapon in the dark, without looking at it in order for me to be the best fighting man possible.

In that moment of truth, when the evil criminal is holding a gun on you and forcing you to kneel and turn away from him, your heart will be beating so fast, that all you'll have left to fall back on is your training. And, if you've got no training, then ... hence the phrase "You'll die in a puddle of your own blood, puke and urine."

Almost every day I log into my computer and I go to YouTube.com. Then I type in Active Self Protection. I then watch several videos of real-life video surveillance self-defense incidents. It's free training, and it does two things for me.

1. It shows me what a real gunfight looks like. Or a real carjacking or a real knife attack. It's not like Hollywood. It's not like your imagination. It is a moment of terror. It can be the greatest moment of your life, or it can be the last moment of your life. You get to choose.

"To train or not to train, that is the question."

2. It shows me what I have to do to plan for that particular type of attack. John Correia, the host and creator of Active Self Protection gives you the tactical analysis. What did they do right, what did they do wrong, what should you do in that situation? Ask the questions now, because you won't have the ability, the time and the proper frame of mind to make those decisions in the heat of battle.

John says that in order to survive the attack, you must have the proper attitude, the proper skills and the proper plan. And I agree with him. But here's the rub, folks. You don't get those things simply by buying a gun and getting a permit. You don't get a trophy simply for showing up and entering the race. This is real life, not some artificial fantasy world where everyone who competes wins.

> *"This is a gun fight. And in real life, there is one winner and one loser."*

The person who scores the first critical hit is the one most likely to win the gun fight. And critical hit is defined as any hit to a major organ or the central nervous system. (Reference my book *Civilian Combat* for more details on how to do that.)

> *One percent is pitiful and it's scary.*

In all reality, what it means is that 99 percent of those who carry for personal protection are poorly trained. No one who ever came out of a gun fight was heard to say:

> *"Oh. man. I just wish I'd had less ammo."*

By the same token, no one ever came out of a gun fight saying:

> *"Oh. man. I just wish I'd had less training."*

In the end, that slight and precarious moment before bullets enter your body, you'll want several things:

- more ammo
- body armor
- more firepower
- several of your friends

And last, but certainly not least, you'll want more training, so you can withstand the fiery bullets of the devil.

"Since the dawn of mankind, humans have had to rely on their thinking prowess to survive. The firearm is merely the means to attain the end."

— *Louis Awerbuck*

"A warrior who is prepared to fight must also be prepared to die."

— *Sun Tzu*

"Anyone who gets in a fair fight...has no tactical skills."

— *Anonymous*

"Courage is being scared to death and saddling up anyway."

— *John Wayne*

"Cowards die many times before their deaths; The valiant never taste of death but once."

— *William Shakespeare*

"The more thou sweateth in training, the less thou bleedeth in combat."

— *Richard Marcinko, Seal Team 6*

The wolf cares not, how many the sheep be."

— *Plato*

Helpful Resources

Here are some very good trainers whom I highly recommend:

John Correia, Active Self Protection
www.activeselfprotection.com

Rob Pincus, ICE Training Inc.
www.icetraining.us

Massad Ayoob, Massad Ayoob Group
www.massadayoob.com

Gabe Suarez, Suarez International
www.suarezinternational.com

Dave Spaulding, Handgun Combatives, Inc
www.handguncombatives.com

Bob Houzenga & Andy Kemp, Midwest Training Group
www.midwesttraininggroup.net

Here I am with Lieutenant General Jerry Boykin (retired) at Cornerstone University. The general is a founding member of Delta Force and later became the commanding general of the Special Operations Command. Presently he is the Executive Vice President of the Family Research Council. I was honored to be on the general's personal security detail several times as he toured, speaking about the dangers of Islamic terrorism. I learned very quickly that he enjoyed teasing Marines. That's okay, because I was quick to tease him back. He's a very good man.

This picture was taken in Chicago, Illinois at a class taught by Massad Ayoob called "*Judicious Use of Deadly Force*". It was 20 hours of intensive training on the legal and emotional ramifications of being involved in a lethal shoot-out. The Massad Ayoob Group gives some of the best training in the world. You should make time to train with Massad. Massad is the master. (Go to www.ayoob.com for info on his classes.) Two friends and MAG Instructors, Bob Houzenga and Andy Kemp, are kneeling in the front row.

Massad is kneeling in the number one spot and I am standing behind him. Andy and Bob are kneeling in the number 4 and 5 positions, respectively.

(Photo courtesy of Vernon Jenewein)

Midwest Tactical teaches all across Michigan, but our home range is here in Hastings at the Barry County Conservation Club. We also teach in Hamilton Rod & Gun Club, Fennville Rod & Gun Club, and Centershot Indoor Gun Range in Dorr, MI.

(Photo courtesy of Jared Fulton)

After two days of Combat Focus Shooting class, we posed for the camera with Instructor Rob Pincus. I enjoy Rob's training. What he teaches makes sense to me, and I try to pass it on to my own students whenever possible.

Here I am with Kathy Jackson, firearms instructor and author of "The Cornered Cat: A Women's Guide to Concealed Carry." I am proud to serve as Kathy's publisher. Her book has been our #1 best seller for 5 years running. Kathy is a great ambassador to the cause, bringing in and training women shooters all over the country.

As an author, publisher, and USCCA firearms instructor, I get to spend time with some great people in the firearms industry. Here are Tim Schmidt, founder of the United States Concealed Carry Association, and Mark Walters, host of Armed American Radio. Both are friends and men of great character. Tim is the slightly taller gentleman on the right. The guy's a beanstalk!

Here I am with two of my funniest Second Amendment friends.
Kenn Blanchard on the left is also one of my authors who wrote
"Black Man with a Gun: Reloaded." Rick Ector on my right is
a fellow concealed carry instructor teaching in Detroit at Rick's
Firearms Academy.

In the past 30 years I've introduced all my children to firearms. I enjoy teaching them to be safe and how to protect themselves and their family.

Nathan Nephew is on the left and Brian Jeffs is on the right of me. Brian and Nate are co-founders of Michigan Open Carry as well as co-authors of the book *My Parents Open Carry*. I serve with them on the Board of Directors for the group I founded called The Second Amendment March. Guys like this make it fun to fight for the right to keep and bear arms.

Here I am with my friend and fellow instructor Joel Fulton as we review his comments on my manuscript. The two of us have been training civilians and fighting for the right to keep and bear arms for many years. Joel co-owns Freedom Firearms in Battle Creek, Michigan with his brother Jared. It's an excellent gun store and indoor range. If you are ever in the area, be sure to stop in and say hello.

Skip is behind the microphone at iHeart Radio in Grand Rapids, Michigan. Skip is co-host for the largest military veteran talk show in America, which is syndicated on well over 250 stations. Check it out at frontlinesoffreedom.com.

Skip in the studio with friend, fellow author and radio personality, Rick Vuyst. Rick has been the host of the award-winning Flowerland Garden Show for 25 years running. Rick is the author of *I just Wet My Plants* and his latest book *Operation Rumination*. Go to myflowerland.com to learn more about Rick.

Host of Frontlines of Freedom, Colonel Denny Gillem, and co-host Skip Coryell, as we accept the Michigan Association of Broadcast award for best show in category for 2018.

Skip Coryell at the Second Amendment March with Lt. Governor Brian Calley and Barry County Sheriff Dar Leaf. The Second Amendment March is held each year at the state capitol. You can find out more by going to secondamendment-march.com. See you there!

By nature, training for warfighting can cause imbalance ... Spiritual fitness is an important component of holistic well-being.

The Official Website of the
United States Marine Corps

Chapter 9

Spiritual Fitness

THERE ARE TWO KINDS OF PEOPLE in this world: those who pass Algebra class, and those who flunk. I flunked Algebra three times. And I've sometimes wondered, "Was I incredibly stupid or was I wonderfully resilient?" In retrospect, I think I was a little of both. And I suspect that people who have the internal strength (stubbornness) to take Algebra three times are also the ones who do well in Marine Corps boot camp. I hated boot camp, but it wasn't all that different than living at home, at least on an emotional level. On a physical level, yeah, it was really tough. But I made it through and it changed me forever. Boot camp is one of those things you're glad you did, but even more glad you'll never have to do it again. I suppose the same can be said for many childhoods.

I still remember vividly the morning of December 29th, 1975. I was 18 years old, and it was snowy and very cold. I remember seeing steam from my breath as I walked to the car to be taken to the airport in Battle Creek, Michigan. (The previous night I had run my dad's car into a ditch and put a dent in the bumper. Very carefully, I covered it with snow, and he didn't discover it until I was safely on board the plane.) Oddly enough, I was in a hurry to go to boot camp, so I wouldn't have to face my dad's wrath at denting his car.

Aside from a few weeks at summer camp, I had never been away from my family before, and I was scared to death. I was homesick already. I had left the state of Michigan only one other time, and that was on a family vacation to visit my Uncle Austin in New York 15 years earlier. But now I was on my own.

I said my good byes. I think Mom was crying, but I don't remember for sure, and then I got on board this little two-engine prop plane just in time for a small blizzard. The plane made it safely to Chicago, where I boarded a jet for San Diego. That was the last time I saw snow for almost a year.

> San Diego was warm and beautiful, and I thought "Hey, maybe boot camp won't be so bad after all."

When the plane landed in San Diego, it was already dark. But I remember the warmth hitting my face as soon as I stepped outside. We were immediately loaded onto a bus, I think it was a pukey green color, and driven to the Marine Corps Recruit Depot. The short drive was very quiet and peaceful in the middle of the night, and although I was still scared, I remember thinking, "Hey, this may not be so bad after all." It was on that bus ride that I saw my very first palm tree, surrounded by concrete and lit up with neon light.

But then the bus pulled into the base and all hell broke loose. "Move it! Move it! Move it!" I met the four people who were going to dominate my life and change me forever. Sergeant O'Neil: "Get outta there you maggot!" Sergeant Mar: "Come on you little turd! Move it faster!" Gunnery Sergeant Preston: "You better be movin' there you little faggot!," and, last, but certainly not least, Platoon Commander, Staff Sergeant Tarver: He just stood there and smiled like Lex Luthor holding a bag of Kryptonite. I had taken my first step into a larger world.

In the dead of night, they herded us like cattle onto a parade deck and made us line up on the cement. I guess the big difference between fathers and Marine Corps Drill Instructors is this: my father had always stopped short of killing me, but I wasn't so sure about these guys. They were Jack Nicholson, Charles Manson, and the Incredible Hulk all rolled into one.

> That first night we didn't sleep, as they herded us like cattle all across the base.

It must have been 10 or 11 PM when we arrived, but they didn't let us sleep. Instead, they marched us all over the base for the rest of the night. They took away our civilian clothes and gave us new ones. In fact, they issued us all kinds of green stuff, which I later learned was correctly called olive drab. They issued us black, leather, military boots which didn't fit. (To this day, my feet are little more than clubs, which I use as props to hold myself up.) And then at 6AM (I'm sorry, I mean zero six hundred hours) when we were all emotionally and physically exhausted, they shaved off my beautiful, long, blonde hair, in less than 30 seconds. I felt like a bowling ball with eyes. Without my hair, I was no longer a person. I was totally dehumanized.

Finally, they took us to experience our first Marine Corps breakfast. I still remember those, big, heavy, stainless steel eating trays. I was starving, so I filled it up as high as I could pile it with scrambled eggs, pancakes, fruit, cottage cheese (for some reason they served cottage cheese at all meals) orange juice, milk, and some kind of white meat sauce that I never identified. I sat down at the table, took 15 seconds to pray, then lifted the heavily laden fork to my lips.

"Move it! Move it! Move it! Get outside! Now! Let's go ladies! Let's go!" I couldn't believe my ears. They had given 88 people only 15 minutes to get through the line and eat. Very few of us consumed any of our meal that morning or the next few meals to follow. But within a few days, all of us had learned to inhale our food in a matter of seconds, sucking up the nutrients like a wet-dry shop vac.

> They gave 88 recruits less than 15 minutes to get through line and eat.

In Marine Corps boot camp a series is composed of four platoons, and a platoon is composed of approximately 80 recruits. My platoon number was 1001, as we were the first platoon formed in the Marine Corps for the year of 1976 in San Diego, California. I was in Marine Corps boot camp for a total of 13 weeks. Eleven weeks is the norm, but we had to train an extra two weeks while waiting for the other three platoons to arrive and form. Marine Corps boot camp was tough, tougher than anything else I've done, though emotionally similar to my childhood and my first two marriages.

I remember as a child, growing up in the sixties and early seventies, watching the Vietnam War on television with my father. He always watched television, especially the 6 o'clock news, with the utmost intensity. It was a cardinal rule in our house: "Under pain of death, never walk between Dad and the television set." I can still hear his gruff, angry voice. "You make a better door than you do a window!" For years I sat on the couch, not moving, watching them unload wounded and dead bodies from the Huey helicopters. All the while, my father would lecture me on the evils of communism, how they had to be stopped before they took over the world. I didn't understand his obsession then, but, in retrospect, it all makes sense. He had fought the massive hordes of Chinese Communists in Korea, and it had shaped him forever. He was afraid of them.

> When I turned 18, I would enlist and go fight for my country. The thought terrified me to my core.

Part of the reason I joined the Marine Corps was to make my father proud of me; that part worked. He was proud, very proud. But another reason was flat-out guilt at missing the Vietnam War. Since I grew up watching it on television, I also grew up knowing in my heart of hearts that I would be sent to fight in that war. It was a given. When I turned 18, I would enlist and go fight for my country. The thought terrified me to my core.

I recall the happy/sad day in Spring of 1975 when the communists marched into Saigon. I was just finishing my senior year in high school, and I remember the sense of relief I felt, knowing that I wasn't going to die in a rice paddy in some far-off land. Later, I felt ashamed of my cowardice. Throughout the years, I have developed a keen sense of respect and admiration for Vietnam veterans, even to the point of identifying with them. The military does that to you; develops a keen and overwhelming instinct inside the individual for country and corps. Eventually, I developed a mild case of survivor's guilt, because I was supposed to fight and I had not. I had been too young. To this day a mild guilt still lingers.

> In the dead of night, I made my pact with God. Get me through this and I'll serve you to the end of my days.

But in January of 1976 I had bigger problems. These drill instructors were maniacs! They hated me. They were going to kill me. How was I going to make it through the next 13 weeks? The answer came from a most unexpected place.

Every other night or so I pulled guard duty, and I loved it. I suppose that sounds odd, but there has always been something about the still of the night that has drawn me to it. I love to be awake while others are asleep. I feel closer to God when that happens. There are no distractions, no conflict, no confrontation, nothing but stillness, silence and the dead of night. And it was there, walking up and down the aisles of the squad bay, where I made a deal with God. "God, you help me get through this thing, and I'll serve you the rest of my days." It was very simple, nothing profound or complex. I had just come to the end of myself, and, as luck would have it, there I found God. He'd been waiting there all along. Who would have thought that God had been waiting for me in Marine Corps boot camp? It's always the last place you look.

> *"Be still, and know that I am God! I will be honored by every nation. I will be honored throughout the world."*
>
> *Psalm 46:10 (NLT)*

There was no free time in boot camp except for 3 hours on Sunday morning. Looking back, it was a bit humorous the way the drill instructors handled it. They would say: "You now have 3 hours of free time, and during that free time, you will shine your brass, shine your boots, do your laundry, study your general orders . . . ." etc., etc., so on and so forth. To an 18-year-old boy away from home for the first time, drill instructors felt like God. But quickly, I learned that not even a drill instructor could prevent a recruit from going to church on Sunday morning. It was awesome! Once a week for an hour, I could talk and sing and pray without fear of retribution.

> I found God in Marine Corps boot camp; it's always the last place you look.

That probably sounds funny, but you have to understand that Marine Corps boot camp is a whole nuther world. They had us captive in this big, plastic bubble (olive drab in color of course) and they could do anything they wanted to us. And they usually did. I remember the rigid way they made us speak. "Sir, Private Coryell requests permission to speak, sir!" And we always had to yell it out as loud as we could or they would ridicule us into oblivion (because, of course, they were sadists). "What do you want you little shit stain! Drop down and give me some push ups!" To which I would reply. "Sir, how many, sir?" To which they would reply with that sadistic grin, "Forever!"

I remember one time I requested mass with the Chaplain. (In the Marine Corps, any Marine may request an audience with his superior officer and it must be granted.) The Chaplain was a captain. To all you civilians out there, that means that we had to salute him, and, more importantly, drill Instructors had to salute him as well. And this man spoke to me as if I was a real human being. He didn't call me slime or maggot or turd. He looked into my eyes and smiled and said, "It's okay, son. You can talk to me any way you want. Just tell me what's on your mind." I did. I told him how tough it was, that I wasn't sure I could make it through all this. He encouraged me and then prayed for me. He gave me a tiny, green Gideon Bible and reassured me that my drill instructors were not allowed to take it away. I took that Bible with me everywhere. It fit in my breast pocket, and the drill instructors never knew I had it. In boot camp we had the saying "Hurry up and wait!" I never understood why they made us run everywhere, then we would stand outside in formation and wait. In retrospect, I realize that everything they did had a purpose; they just

> The captain didn't call me slime or maggot. He treated me like I was a real human being.

weren't sharing the game plan with us. Whenever we waited, I would sneak out my little, green Bible and read. It wasn't the whole Bible, just the New Testament and Psalms, but I found it incredibly comforting to read about King David crying out to God in his time of need. I felt akin to him, and the loving words of Jesus soothed my heart as well. But my favorite time to read was in the dead of night while on guard duty, standing in the corner of the squad bay closest to the mercury bulb out over the parade deck. It was risky, but that was my only time alone with God. So I took the risk.

Here is one of my favorite verses from that period my life:

> *1 God is our refuge and strength,*
> *A very present help in trouble.*

Psalms 46:1 (NIV)

Back in 1976, I was in a constant state of trouble, always striving, always on alert, always giving a hundred percent and beyond just to make it through the next minute. And I needed God more than ever. It's ironic that boot camp taught me both pride and humility simultaneously.

There were many of us who didn't graduate from boot camp with platoon 1001, and some who didn't graduate at all. We started with 88 recruits, and when we finished 13 weeks later, there were fewer than half of the original group left.

> **Fewer than half of our original platoon graduated as part of platoon 1001.**

On any given day, we never knew who would be weeded out next, and we never assumed we would last through the day. My philosophy was: if they don't notice me, then I can't get in any trouble. For the most part, that strategy worked. I never got in any trouble, but neither did I excel. If I had it all to do over again (and thank God I don't) I would have taken the risk and tried to stand out. The ones who did that, either succeeded, or crashed and burned on the parade deck. It was never pretty.

I remember one person in particular. He had gone to sick call and gotten a prescription medication for a cold. The pressure and stress had become too much for him, so he took the whole bottle of pills. I was surprised at the reaction of my drill instructors. Here was an 18-year-old boy, foaming at the mouth, afraid, depressed, and barely cognizant of what was happening around him. In civilian life, he would have been treated with the utmost care and delicacy, but Sergeant Mar (he was 6 foot 6 and built like a mountain) Sergeant O'Neil, and Gunnery Sergeant Preston all gathered around him, got six inches from his face and began screaming at him. "You're going to jail boy! It's against the law to damage Marine Corps property!

> He was foaming at the mouth, afraid, depressed, and barely cognizant.

Don't you eyeball me boy! Stand at attention! Arms at your side! Shoulders back! Eyes to the front!"

The rest of the platoon stood on our foot lockers at the position of attention, eyes straight ahead, terrified of the lunatics who were in charge of us. But I kept sneaking glimpses of that poor recruit. Within 15 minutes two military police officers came, handcuffed him and drug him out of the squad bay. We never saw him again, and to this day I have no idea if he's alive or dead.

About a month into our training, our numbers were becoming depleted. I remember the first few weeks we had PT (physical training) we were followed by an ambulance every time we ran. Eventually, someone would fall behind, and if they couldn't catch back up, the ambulance scooped them up and hauled them away and we would never see that particular recruit again. I always wondered what they were doing to these guys. (I had read the novel *Soylent Green* in high school and I couldn't get it off my mind.) Were they shooting them? Were we eating them in the hash? I didn't know until about 5 weeks into our training. Right about then new recruits started showing up and were added to our numbers. From them we discovered a little more about how things operated.

I remember Private Strang. He was tall, skinny, and he couldn't do even three pull ups. When Private Strang joined platoon 1001, he had already been in Marine Corps boot camp for close to a year. I was amazed that anyone could endure boot camp for that long, so he gained my immediate respect and sympathy.

> Private Strang spent a year in boot camp. But he never gave up and graduated with us.

From Private Strang we learned the following: All the ones who dropped out during PT were set back in their training, and were picked up by later platoons. He told us about the "bad boy" platoon. That's where they sent recruits who were in need of an attitude adjustment. I remember marching by the bad boy platoon one day. It seemed surreal to watch all those

Marine Corps recruits, chained together in shackles, breaking concrete with sledge hammers. I think the drill instructors marched us by them on purpose, for our own good of course, strictly to show us what would happen if we ever disobeyed. And then there was the "motivational" Platoon. This platoon was composed of recruits who just couldn't quite make the grade without extra help. We called them "the slow class." And, last, but certainly not least, we had the "fat body" platoon. They did a lot of exercise and didn't eat much.

We had all kinds of people in our platoon: black inner city guys, Hispanics, white farm boys, even a few blue bloods, but the drill instructors treated us all the same. Marine Corps boot camp, as far as I could tell, was truly color blind. We were all just different shades of olive drab.

> I never turned my back on Private Sharkey. He was a scary SOB.

I still remember Private Sharkey. He was pretty cocky and full of himself. He used to sit on his footlocker, shining his boots with a smile on his face, all the while saying: "Isn't this great! We're going to be Marines, and as soon as we graduate, we get to kill people! Imagine that, getting paid to kill!" I never turned my back on Private Sharkey. I suspect he's probably in prison somewhere, still shining his boots with a smile on his face, all the while saying: "I was a Marine. It was great! They paid me to kill people." I sometimes wonder if he ever managed to distinguish between peacetime and war.

One of the daily highlights for me was mail call, and I have my mother to thank for that. She wrote me a letter every single day I was in boot camp, telling me what was happening with the family, who was sick, who was healthy, who was in trouble, who was not; it was my daily vitamin shot and it helped me get through the tough times.

I remember that I had a girlfriend when I left. I was 18 and she was only 15. She was the first girl I ever dated, and I was infatuated beyond repair. When I said good bye to her the day before I left, I said to her "Well, absence makes the heart grow fonder." But her parting words confused me. She said, "Out of sight – out of mind." I got two letters from her the entire 6 months I was away. When I returned home, I learned she had another boyfriend. In retrospect, it makes sense, but, at the time, it hurt like hell.

> Entering boot camp I weighed 135 pounds. Upon graduation I was 175 pounds of muscle.

Finally, in early April of 1976, I, along with Private Strang and about 80 other recruits became United States Marines. It was a good feeling. I had made it. Thirteen weeks earlier, I had been a scrawny, 135-pound kid with long hair and no discipline. Now, I was straight as a rod, bristling with muscle and weighed in at 175 pounds. That was over 40 years ago, and I've never been in that good a shape, nor will I ever again. It just hurts too darn much getting that way.

On graduation day, I was surprised to listen to Platoon Commander Staff Sergeant Tarver speak to us with fondness and with a tear in his eye. He congratulated us, thanked us, and called us Marines. (To this day, I still cry during the closing minutes of the movie *Officer and a Gentleman*.)

But what does Marine Corps boot camp have to do with concealed carry and with Christianity?

Spiritual fitness.

Humanity is mortal. We are finite. Our bodies will live and die, because everything that has a beginning ... has an ending. And none of us know when that ending will occur. It could be today, tomorrow, or 10 years from now. But it will happen, and it's not likely to be a time and place of your choosing.

Sure, our souls live on, but the body does not.

> *"By the sweat of your brow you will eat your*
> *food until you return to the ground, since*
> *from it you were taken; for dust you are and*
> *to dust you will return."*
>
> *Genesis 3:19 (NIV)*

Fast forward to today. I'm sitting in my Honda Pilot, in my driveway just a few feet from my house. I always park right in front of the picture window so I can look in and watch my wife and three children as they do the home school thing. I guess I'm still on guard duty, just like I was in the Marines. My wife is in there right now, talking to my 13-year-old son. I get a warm feeling when I watch my family, knowing they are okay, that I can still protect them, that I can walk into the house and partake of their love. And I do that quite often.

But here's the rub. Our lives are fleeting; they can end at any time.

> *13 Now listen, you who say, "Today or*
> *tomorrow we will go to this or that city,*
> *spend a year there, carry on business and*
> *make money." 14 Why, you do not even*
> *know what will happen tomorrow. What is*

your life? You are a mist that appears for a
little while and then vanishes. 15 Instead,
you ought to say, "If it is the Lord's will, we
will live and do this or that."

James 4:13-15(NIV)

We are humans living in a dangerous world. We exist and move and have our being simply by the good graces of our God. We are but a vapor that quickly rises up in the morning and then is extinguished by the heat of the sun.

And that is why spiritual fitness is of the utmost importance, not just for people who carry guns, but for all of us. Examine your life every day. Do you have things that need to be said to your loved ones? Do you need to apologize to someone you've wronged? Do you need to lend forgiveness to someone who has wronged you? If so, best to get it done before the sun rises and turns the vapor into nothingness.

And, most of all, get right before your God. Because, sooner or later, you're going to meet your maker. The Marine Corps made me physically fit, but, spiritual fitness is more important. The body wastes away, but the spirit lasts forever.

26 What good will it be for someone to gain
the whole world, yet forfeit their soul? Or
what can anyone give in exchange for their
soul?

Matthew 16:26 (NIV)

Things to Remember

1. Surrender is a choice. Choose to fight on.

2. Push yourself to your limits, and then go another ten percent.

3. Warriors are not born - they are made through pain and toil and blood and sweat.

4. Training is everything. You can't get enough of it. Always upgrade. Be happy, but never be satisfied with your present level of expertise.

5. Be a Marine in attitude and mindset.

6. You already have an appointment with God. Always be spiritually prepared to meet Him.

"They're on our right; they're on our left; they're in front of us; they're behind us. They can't get away now!"

Colonel Chesty Puller, USMC

Read this inspirational and uplifting book of stories about real life and find out why Laughter and tears are truly the medicinal balm of life. They both heal, empower, and exhort, but they were created to be mutually inclusive. They are two sides of the same coin. To have one and not the other is to go through life with a lopsided personality. All tears and you may end up hopelessly bitter and morose. Conversely, too much laughter, and you may dance through life, never growing wise, never grappling with the eternal questions of Why . Laughter and tears are beautiful gifts from God. Liken them to a pair of wonderful shoes. If you wear one, without the other, the best you can hope for is to limp along through life, doing less than what God intended for you. But if you can merge the two, incorporate both of them appropriately into your life, then you will be freed to live life fully and to better serve others. And now, I wish you the best, as you laugh and cry your way through God s gift of life.

You look like the Pillsbury Dough-boy. If I poke your stomach, will it make you laugh...? We're gonna have to make some room for your lunch, Bacon-boy! Get down there and give me 25 crunches. AND COUNT THEM OUT!

– Major Payne

Chapter 10

Physical Fitness

THESE DAYS I'M TEACHING MORE and more advanced concealed carry classes. I enjoy those classes more than the introductory level classes, simply because the students are there because they want to be there, because they are serious about honing their personal-protection skills, and not because the government is requiring it as a prerequisite to getting a concealed pistol license. These classes are smaller, and I get to know the students on a personal level, simply because we spend 8 hours shooting on a range, and because the classes are only about six students. I like that.

But some of my students, both in basic and advanced classes, are overweight, some grossly so. It's sad for me to watch a man grunt and groan as he tries to bend down and retrieve a magazine. On the one hand, I applaud that he's still active, and that he's trying to better himself and learn more about protecting himself and his family; however, on the other hand, this person's greatest danger isn't death from mugging or a mass shooter; his greatest risk is from metabolic disease.

According to the Mayo Clinic website:

> *Metabolic syndrome is a cluster of conditions that occur together, increasing your risk of heart disease, stroke and type 2 diabetes. These conditions include increased blood pressure, high blood sugar, excess body fat around the waist, and abnormal cholesterol or triglyceride levels.*

Let's face it folks, if we live long enough, most of us will have to deal with unwanted weight gain. It's just one of those inevitable things that go with old age. Longevity is a good thing, but it's also a package deal; it comes with strings attached.

Right now I'm sitting in my hometown cemetery. I come here often while working on books. It's a peaceful place, simply because the residents don't bother me. It's a very quiet neighborhood here at Oak Hill Resort and Cemetery. But I understand that a lot these people didn't have to die at such a young age. Some of their deaths were self-inflicted. They were overweight and out of shape, which, in itself, is a form of time-released suicide.

Before coming here, I stopped off at McDonald's for breakfast and bought a low-fat, sugar-free vanilla latte. But that's not what I wanted to buy. I wanted the McDonald's Big Breakfast with hotcakes and a large Coke. So why did I spend good money on something I didn't really want? Well, quite frankly, I'm drinking the sugar-free latte to avoid becoming a fat pig. Let me tell you a story.

Back in my younger days, I was 20, still in the Marine Corps Reserves, playing varsity soccer at college, in my prime, young and strong and fast. I could run forever and I did. I enjoyed exercise. I remember waking up in the morning and feeling sore, and asking myself, "why do I hurt today?" But there was always a good answer. "Oh yes, I ran 6 miles yesterday."

Fast-forward to today. Now I'm 61 years old, and I wake up in the morning, and my bones ache; my joints ache, my muscles and tendons ache. And I ask myself: why do I hurt so much? And then I remember. Oh yes, it's because I'm 61 years old, and still pumping blood and breathing oxygen. The French philosopher and mathematician Rene Descartes said:

"Cogito, ergo sum."

That's the Latin, but the English translation is "I think, therefore I am." The 61-year-old version of Skip Coryell has modified that profundity just a tad:

"I hurt, therefore I am."

I have no idea what that is in Latin, but, of course, they are both true. However, the pain is what really gets my attention more than the thinking. Any fool can think, and it's much easier to get fat than it is to stay fit. Getting fat is effortless. All you have to do is relax, and allow the immutable and unforgiving law of entropy to take charge. What is the law of entropy?

entropy - [en-truh-pee]

> *Noun- The idea of entropy comes from a*
> *principle of thermodynamics dealing with*
> *energy. It usually refers to the idea that*

everything in the universe eventually moves
from order to disorder, and entropy is the
measurement of that change.

Order to disorder. That reminds me of William Butler Yeats, an Irish poet, dramatist, and essayist, who won the Nobel prize in 1923. His most famous poem alluded to entropy. It was titled *The Second Coming.* Here is an excerpt:

Turning and turning in the widening gyre
The falcon cannot hear the falconer;
Things fall apart; the centre cannot hold;
Mere anarchy is loosed upon the world,

The blood-dimmed tide is loosed, and
everywhere
The ceremony of innocence is drowned;
The best lack all conviction, while the worst
Are full of passionate intensity.

Things fall apart ... the center does cannot hold. Well, folks, I'm not as profound or cerebral as Yeats, but I do understand the correlation: The center does not hold ... and neither does the waistline.

Once you reach a certain age, and, it's different for all of us, you will be forever fighting entropy. Gravity is unrelenting; it never goes away, is always there, working, pulling you down, and you will always find yourself with a choice:

I can fight

or

I can let myself go.

My most sincere advice to you is this: Don't let yourself go. Don't stop fighting gravity. Do not relent to age. Never give up. Never give in. Never surrender. Old age will come all too soon. Don't hasten its arrival by drinking and eating with wild abandon.

I know I'm not supposed to call people fat, so I'll say it a different way ... there's a severe shortage of skinny people in America.

One of my favorite firearms instructors is Gabe Suarez out of Arizona. I've interviewed Gabe many times on *The Home Defense Show*, and Gabe makes this irrefutable statement about personal fitness:

> *"Healthy, fit people fight better and are harder to kill."*

Check out Gabe Suarez at suarezinternational.com or go on his YouTube channel. Gabe is approaching 60 years old, but he still works out and stays in shape. Gabe is proof that you don't have to let yourself go, that you can fight the ravages of time. You can't stop them, but you can slow entropy down a bit.

Another firearms instructor who encourages me is John Correia. John was overweight; there's no other way to put it. But John recognized the problem and lost a lot of inches off his waistline, and now he teaches personal defense all over America. Check out his YouTube channel called *Active Self Protection*. John now has over 1.3 million subscribers to his channel, and it's getting bigger every day.

Both these men inspire me to become better, to not give up and never give in. Accountability is important, and that's why this is one of my favorite verses in the entire Bible:

> *17 As iron sharpens iron,*
> *so one person sharpens another.*

> *Proverbs 27:17 (NIV)*

What exactly does it mean to sharpen iron? Sharpening iron is not an easy thing. You have to cause friction and heat. You are filing away, through active, intentional effort, tiny bits of metal, honing yourself to a fine edge. This doesn't come naturally. You are working intentionally against the ravages of time, entropy and gravity.

So, how do you accomplish this? How do you hone your body into a physically fit tool of personal defense?

You work.

I wish there was an easier way ... oh, God help me I wish there was an easier way. I've tried all kinds of diets, but, while they may work at the beginning, your body returns to its set weight once you go off the diet. Concealed carry is a lifestyle, and so is staying in shape. You have to develop a personal system that works for you.

Here are some of the things that work for me:

1. Stay away from sugar. Sugar is like Kryptonite to me. How one ounce of sugar directly translates into one pound of fat is beyond me. But don't fool yourself. Sugar is an addictive substance, and getting off it is hard and takes will power and work.

2. Eat protein. Stay with lean meat like wild game, fish, chicken and turkey. They are low in fat and carbohydrates, and they also contribute to muscle development. Muscle burns more calories than fat, so

do some weight training as well as cardio-vascular workouts. Remember, the stronger you are, the better you can fight off attackers. The average person can fight hard for about 15 seconds, but if you're out of shape, you may last only five.

3. Cardio. Run and walk everyday. Get your heart-rate up. Some people die during the gun fight, not by bullet wounds, but by heart attack. They get that adrenaline dump into their bloodstream, and their heart rates sky rocket. And if your heart can't handle it, well, then it's a very short gun fight. You die in a puddle of your own blood, puke and urine.

4. Count your calories. Part of successful weight loss is more accounting than anything else. I have an app on my cell phone that allows me to input everything I eat. It keeps a running total of my daily caloric intake, and lets me know what I can eat throughout the day. It also tells me what foods are best for me, and helps me in my long-range goals.

5. Tell your friends about your weight goals. Make a commitment to yourself, your friends and your family to lose x number of pounds in x amount of time. Then ask them to hold you to it. For me, I announced it on *The Home Defense Show*, and this changed my mindset. I don't want everyone to know I've failed, so I work harder to keep from embarrassing myself.

Here is a basic precept that has helped me in all aspects of my life. Always remember this:

> *"The reason most people fail instead of succeed is they trade what they want most for what they want at the moment."*

> — *Napoleon Bonaparte*

Right now I want a triple cheeseburger from McDonalds. I love those things. And I want a chocolate shake to wash it down. That would be heaven to me. But I'm not going to do it. Why? Because I know if I do, I'll gain weight. And if I gain weight, then several very wonderful and awesome things will **not** happen to me:

1. I won't feel as good physically. My pants will get tight at the waistline. I won't be able to run with my kids, climb into a tree stand to deer hunt, play basketball or airsoft wars with my family.

2. I won't see myself as a success, and I'll lose my self-respect. I want to feel good about myself and the things I accomplish in life.

3. I won't be respected by my friends, family and peers. I don't want them to feel sorry for me; I want them to look up to me and be encouraged and inspired by me.

4. I won't live a long and healthy life. My wife is 20 years younger than I, and I still have three kids at home, two of them under the age of 10. I want to see them grow up. I want to walk my daughter down the aisle. I want to see my sons go to college and succeed in life. I want to be there for my wife, kids and grandkids during those pivotal points in life when they need sage advice.

One of the saddest things about old age is this: I've spent an entire lifetime gaining knowledge, wisdom born of pain, and just now, when I finally have some great things to offer the world, my body gives up on me. I don't like it, and, quite frankly, it makes me a bit frustrated.

But here's the bottom line folks: your body may give up on you, but never give up on your body. Always work. Always fight. Do everything you can to stay in shape and become a better fighter, protector and defender.

To you old folks out there. Start out slow, but gradually increase your workouts. The best way to lose weight is to eat less and exercise more.

Lest you young folks get cocky, remember this. Your grandfather is your future. You will not always be young. Your life is but a vapor. It's much easier to keep from gaining weight than it is to burn it off after it's on. The lifestyle you develop now, when you're young, will stay with you into your middle-age. Your metabolism will slow down gradually and sneak up on you by age 30. Don't let it do that. People who are failing to plan are also planning to fail.

> *"Healthy, fit people fight better and are harder to kill."*
>
> *– Gabe Suarez*

Plan for health. Work for health.

> *15. A sluggard buries his hand in the dish; he is too lazy to bring it back to his mouth.*
>
> *Proverbs 26:15 (NIV)*

Things to Remember

1. Being out of shape can kill you as fast as a 160-grain hollow point.

2. Start an exercise program. Stick to it and never give up!

3. Eat smart and healthy. Keep your weight down or you may die in a puddle of your own blood, puke and urine.

   "Healthy, fit people fight better and are harder to kill."

   – Gabe Suarez

Suddenly, the lights went out, not just in one town or village, but all across the world. It was an act of cyber terrorism that plunged the world into the heart of darkness, into the 1000-year night, letting loose the demons of a billion souls, pitting dark against light, causing each person everywhere to choose sides. Not since Stephen King's "The Stand" has there been an apocalyptic thriller of such epic proportions. Read book one of this 3-book series and see what happens when society's thin veneer of civility is stripped away. "The God Virus" is gripping, seething and oozing with the best and worst humanity has to offer.

ACTIVE SELF

PROTECTION
ATTITUDE . SKILLS . PLAN

Active Self Protection is a YouTube channel with well over 1.3 million subscribers. The channel is run by John Correia, and is an incredible personal defense training tool for all concealed carriers. Every day John posts a new video of a real-life personal defense encounter and trains us in how we can defend in a similar scenario should it happen to us. I watch John's videos every week and consider it a vital part of my own personal defense training. Go to YouTube.com right now and subscribe to Active Self Protection. The training you receive will make you better prepared to protect and defend the ones you love!

– Skip Coryell

These days there are a lot of companies out there who want to sell you personal protection insurance, but Firearms Legal Protection (FLP) is the only one I trust to protect myself and my family. Most of my students worry about the ramifications of using deadly force in self-protection, but it doesn't have to be that way. With a membership in FLP, you can carry with confidence, knowing that you have a powerful, legal ally on your side. They have a vast network of competent attorneys across the country, waiting to help. Join Firearms Legal Protection, and help is just a phone call away!

To learn more go to firearmslegal.com/midwesttactical.

– Skip Coryell

Stupid Juice (noun)

Alcohol. The good stuff. Alcoholic bever-
age that enables one to become more
comfortable/confident in social situations.

Usage: "Yo, let me get a shot of that stupid juice."

– *urbandictionary.com*
by *cacton January 06, 2012*

Chapter 11

Addiction and Self-defense

I CAN STILL VIVIDLY REMEMBER THE ONE and only time I got drunk.

I was living in my brother's garage, sleeping on the greasy cement floor, working three jobs, paying more child support than a body has a right to, eating fried squash, wild mulberries, and collecting potatoes from the muck fields in Orangeville. On that particular night, the pain became so great, that I spent every cent I had on a four-pack of Seagram's Peach Wine Coolers. After work, with every intention of drinking until I passed out, I laid down on the dirty foam pad that I used for a bed, and I watched the Johnny Carson monologue on my little black and white television. After the first bottle, I felt dizzy. The second made it hard to get up. After the third, I could no longer hold my head up. But I have to admit, that Johnny Carson was in great form that evening. Every word he said was funny. I even laughed at the commercial breaks.

I remember that my brother walked in after the third wine cooler, looked down at the bottles on the floor and smiled at me. I had been a staunch anti-drinker my whole life, and he was amused at my predicament. After teasing me for a few minutes, he left and I was alone again - alone with my thoughts, my feelings, my pain. - all the things crux and core to my life – just the basics - all the things that country & western songs talk about.

Oddly enough, I didn't forget my pain that night, and I never drank the last wine cooler. My mind remained as clear as a bell. I just couldn't walk. I blamed God that night, cursing him for my clarity and cognizance, imagining that he was not allowing me to get off so easily. God would not allow me to run from my problems or to drown them in alcohol. Today, I thank Him.

> **After the third wine cooler, Johnny Carson's jokes took on a new level of funny.**

What would have happened to me if the alcohol had worked? I shudder to think of it. And the old saying lingers on: "There, but for the grace of God, go I."

So I thank God that the booze didn't work, that I was unable to anesthetize the pain. I was forced to feel, to think, and to work through it. Isn't it ironic, that my second wife was an alcoholic? I suppose that means something. It would appear that God's plan for my life doesn't include alcohol or any other "easy" way out.

There are many types of addictions, but drug and alcohol abuse are wild cards. Meaning ... they change everything.

My second wife was an alcoholic. She wasn't drinking when we married, but I knew about the problem, and naively thought it was something most people could just stop doing if they wanted to.

I was wrong.

Diana was a binge drinker. She could go for several months without a drink, and then drink for days on end until she decided to stop again. I recall with painful clarity, one particular eye-opening event in my life. She had been drinking for several days, hopping in the car as soon as I got home from work, and then not returning until it was time for me to leave for work the next morning. On that particular night, I'd had enough, but talking seemed to do no good. Nothing I said seemed to deter her. I was holding our one-year-old son in my arms as she hopped into the car to drive away. In desperation, I stood behind the vehicle and told her that if she wanted to drink tonight, then she'd have to run over me to do it. She didn't hesitate.

> That was the moment I realized: she would kill me and our children if I stood between her and the bottle.

She put the car in reverse and slammed her foot down on the accelerator. I was shocked and barely had enough time to jump out of the way. That was the moment I realized: she would kill me and our children if I stood between her and the bottle.

In retrospect, I've come to understand that she did love me, even though she was willing to kill me. Now, that may sound odd to most people. After all, it sounds odd to me, and I'm the one who lived through it. In Diana's heart of hearts, she did love me and she did love our children. But here's the rub. When you are suffering from an addiction, it is an all-consuming passion. You will do almost anything for the next drink, the next fix, the next high. Because you no longer live for yourself. You no longer own yourself. You are simply the host for a deadly pathogen that is slowly killing you.

In order to discuss addiction and self-defense, we must address it from two angles:

1. What does the Bible say about it?

2. How does it affect the concealed carry holder?

The Bible is pretty clear about addiction. No man can serve two masters. And the substance owns you in the most profound and basic way. It alters your mind, and allows you to do things that you normally would cringe upon.

> *"No one can serve two masters. Either*
> *you will hate the one and love the other, or*
> *you will be devoted to the one and despise*
> *the other. You cannot serve both God and*
> *money.*

> *Matthew 6:24 (NIV)*

Of course, addictions come in many forms. A person can become addicted to almost anything: video games, cell phones, work, television, sex, money, food, and even exercise.

God says that you cannot serve two masters, and that's a big problem with addiction. How can you serve God when you are beholden to a bottle or a syringe? You can't. Many people try, but they always fail.

> *21 for drunkards and gluttons become poor,*
> *and drowsiness clothes them in rags.*
>
> *Proverbs 23:21 (NIV)*

> *18 Do not get drunk on wine, which leads to*
> *debauchery. Instead, be filled with the Spirit,*
>
> *Ephesians 5:18 (NIV)*

The Bible does not forbid drinking, but I think it's clear that drunkenness can be a major game-changer.

> *9 Or do you not know that wrongdoers will*
> *not inherit the kingdom of God? Do not*
> *be deceived: Neither the sexually immoral*
> *nor idolaters nor adulterers nor men who*
> *have sex with men[a] 10 nor thieves nor the*
> *greedy nor drunkards nor slanderers nor*
> *swindlers will inherit the kingdom of God.*
>
> *1 Corinthians 6:9-10 (NIV)*

Why did the Apostle Paul include drunkards with idolaters and adulterers? Simply put, drunkenness is a form of idolatry. You are now worshipping the bottle, the needle, the syringe, the cell phone or other electronic device. Anything that controls your life and owns your heart and soul is an idol.

If God owns you, then you love and worship Him and only Him. But when you are addicted, then the needle owns you at a most profound and all-encompassing degree. God is a jealous God, and He wants you to give yourself over to Him with all your heart and soul, never holding anything back. But with addiction, you make a conscious decision to choose loyalty to another master every single day of your life.

After divorcing Diana, I went through a period of pain. After that came the anger. Finally, I came to the point where I pitied her and prayed that she would change for the sake of her and our children. Addiction is a living hell.

> *11 As a dog returns to its vomit, so fools repeat their folly.*

> *Proverbs 26:11 (NIV)*

A Few years after our divorce, Diana died of ovarian cancer. Knowing that she had less than a year to live, she changed her life, and became a much better mother to our children. Ironically, the drugs and alcohol she lived for throughout most of her life, were now the only thing that could lessen the pain of the cancer that destroyed her body.

Addiction is a pathogen. Addiction is a deadly cancer ... a form of time-released suicide. Sadly, addiction separates us from God and kills both the body and the soul.

> *28 Do not be afraid of those who kill the body but cannot kill the soul. Rather, be afraid of the One who can destroy both soul and body in hell.*

> *Matthew 10:28 (NIV)*

Okay then, not a lot of good things in the Bible about people who become addicted. So let's talk now about how addictions affect Christians who carry concealed. The most obvious substances are drugs and alcohol. Everyone worth their salt knows that mind-altering drugs and guns do not work and play well together.

140

Drugs, alcohol and guns do not mix.

Most people are smart enough to know that guns and drugs and alcohol don't mix. But some aren't, and I wish this minority of people would not own guns, because they make the rest of us look bad (not to mention the damage they do to the innocent people around them.)

With alcohol, the problem arises when people try to judge for themselves how much alcohol is too much. In my opinion, if you're going to be carrying a gun for personal defense, then one drink may be too much. Alcohol dulls your senses, your reflexes and your reaction time. No one ever becomes a better gun fighter after a few drinks. (They might think they're better, faster, stronger, smarter, and more good looking ... but they're not.) After one drink you may still be legally able to carry your gun, and perhaps even not impaired and physically able to use the gun for personal defense, but usually this is what happens.

1. After the first drink you say to yourself. *I feel fine. My head is clear and I can still focus.* So you have another.

2. After the second drink you say to yourself. *I feel even better now than I did after the first drink.*

So you go ahead and have a third, a fourth, fifth, etc., until you drive away in your car, get pulled over with a blood alcohol content of .03 or .08 or even higher. In many states this is enough to get your concealed pistol license revoked or suspended.

One of the big problems with drugs and alcohol is this: it erodes away your self-control. And God wants you to have self-control.

> 8 Rather, he must be hospitable, one who
> loves what is good, who is self-controlled,
> upright, holy and disciplined.

> *Titus 1:8 (NIV)*

If you decide to drink, then take the firearm out of the mix. Take the time and effort to ensure your firearm is secure in accordance with the laws of your jurisdiction. There's a reason cops call alcohol "stupid juice."

Now let's talk about drug use and guns. During class I'll go around the room and ask students to name off a drug. Most people give answers like this: heroin, meth, LSD, cocaine.

And to be sure these are all very dangerous illegal drugs that should not be mixed with firearms. But many times people focus so much on illegal drugs that they fail to recognize legal drugs as potential safety hazards when coupled with firearms.

Prescription painkillers are an example of this. Many of my students are older, which means they've had back surgery, hip and knee replacements, or arthritis. All of these can cause severe pain requiring strong medication to alleviate the discomfort and enhance mobility. I advise my students on medication to ask their doctor about the possible side effects of the medication. The potential problem here is doctors have lawyers who often advise against taking on any added liability. So when you go to your doctor and say "Hey Doc. Is it okay if I shoot my guns while on this medication?" you may not get a straight answer. However, if you modify your question to be "Hey Doc. Is it okay if I drive a car or operate heavy equipment while on this medication?" Then you're more likely to get a clear, useful answer.

The basic common-sense rule is this: If your senses or judgement are impaired (even a little) then you should not be handling firearms. This could entail something as innocent as an over-the-counter night-time cold medicine with something in it to help you sleep at night. For me, after taking this type of medicine the night before, I'll wake up the next morning feeling drowsy. When this happens I wait a few hours to strap on my firearm, giving me a chance to wake up fully before adding a gun to the mix.

How is your attacker affected by drugs and alcohol?

The answer is quite simple. He will be emboldened. He will lose his self-control, and a part of his humanity will become dead. A person on drugs and alcohol is far more likely to commit a crime than someone who is in their right mind. Someone who is addicted, is under the influence of their drug of choice even when they are sober. That's why my wife tried to run over my son and I when I stood between her and her next high.

The person who attacks you will be numbed, body, mind and spirit, and no longer in their right mind. Their inhibitions will be gone; that's why they're doing something they normally wouldn't do. Of course, habitual addictions, over a long period of time, can result in mental illness as well as flat-out evil. I speak from experience, not as a doctor.

Like mental illness, drugs and alcohol can make your attacker feel invincible and strong. With all inhibitions gone, they are no longer restrained morally or emotionally. All they can think is ... attack, rage, kill.

That makes the person you are most likely to be defending against ... an unrestrained killer. For this reason you may have to shoot many times to stop the threat. Most drugs are also pain killers, so they may not even know you are shooting them.

Bottom Line

Don't be controlled by addictions, and don't associate with those who are.

> *11 But now I am writing to you that you must not associate with anyone who claims to be a brother or sister but is sexually immoral or greedy, an idolater or slanderer, a drunkard or swindler. Do not even eat with such people.*
>
> *1 Corinthians 5:11 (NIV)*

Things to Remember

1. Never step between a drunkard and his drink.

2. Alcohol and guns do not work and play well together.

3. No one can serve two masters.

4. Addiction is a wild card; it changes every thing and everyone it touches.

5. A person under the influence is not in their right mind. They are unrestrained and will commit violence they otherwise would not.

6. Self-control is a fruit of the spirit and should be sought after.

7. Addiction is a deadly cancer that kills both the body and the soul.

8 They all plotted together to come and fight against Jerusalem and stir up trouble against it. 9 But we prayed to our God and posted a guard day and night to meet this threat.

Nehemiah 4:9-10 (NIV)

Chapter 12

Church Safety Teams

DURING **N**EHEMIAH'S **TIME,** **WHILE** rebuilding the wall of Jerusalem, the workers faced an imminent, deadly threat.

16 From that day on, half of my men did the work, while the other half were equipped with spears, shields, bows and armor. The officers posted themselves behind all the people of Judah 17 who were building the wall. Those who carried materials did their work with one hand and held a weapon in the other, 18 and each of the builders wore his sword at his side as he worked.

Nehemiah 4:16-18 (NIV)

The concept of the church safety team seems extreme to many in the church today, but that opinion is rapidly changing. I foresee a time when a church without some type of protection will be considered a foolish oddity.

All throughout recorded human history, physical security has been considered a high priority, and rightly so. The world has always been a dangerous place. To be sure, there are different levels of danger, but danger has been and always will be with us.

Ask someone who is against church security if they lock their doors at night, lock their vehicles, have an alarm system or take any other personal safety precautions, and, if they are honest, they'll tell you "yes." Only a fool would choose to ignore real and credible threats.

The threat to 21st Century Christians is rapidly growing. Gone are the days when criminals honored the house of God as a no-go zone. To the contrary, now they are targeted simply because they are considered soft targets, like schools and places of business. Churches, by virtue of our secularized America, are now considered just another pistol-free zone, to be exploited by mass shooters and other violent criminals.

In the year 2017 there were 118 violent deaths in faith-based institutions across America. The trend is rising, and will continue to rise until churches wake up and take responsibility for guarding the flock. We guard ourselves at home, but refuse to protect those who come into our churches. That attitude is killing people. If you're going to invite the general public into your house of worship, then you have a responsibility to make sure they're safe during their visit.

I have many people on a regular basis tell me they want to form an armed church safety team at their church, but the pastor or the governing body will not allow it. They say "God will protect us." or "The church is a sacred place, and guns don't belong here." Not only is this inconsistent; it's also not true. God is not some magic talisman that protects and defends and wards off evil simply because we pledge our lives to Him. If

148

that were true, then Christians wouldn't need smoke alarms, seat belts, or medical care. But God doesn't serve us ... we serve Him. And the sovereignty of God may seem fickle to us humans, but ... let's face it ... God chooses when to intervene, and when to stand back and let humanity and nature take its course. And as far as guns having no place in the church, tell that to the mass shooters. Good luck with that.

You can depend on God to love you and always be there for you; however, God is not a bullet-proof vest, and shouldn't be reduced to that. God is sovereign. He does as He pleases on a daily and eternal basis. That doesn't mean God doesn't love us or care about us. To the contrary, the Bible and human history is rife with God's acts of love and kindness on the human race. God will give you the strength and courage to do the right thing, but He seldom does the work for you.

> *1 God is our refuge and strength, an ever-present help in trouble. 2 Therefore we will not fear, though the earth give way and the mountains fall into the heart of the sea, 3 though its waters roar and foam and the mountains quake with their surging.*

> *Psalms 46:1-3 (NIV)*

Your children will "probably" not need their seat belts this week, but ... you would be derelict in your duty if you didn't make them buckle up. Your house has probably never burned down, but you'd be a fool to forego fire insurance.

Your church safety team is insurance against the growing possibility of violence at your church. Twentieth and twenty-first century America is not representative of all human history. For the most part we had, and still have, a society that is civil and orderly. The concept of law and order still rules, and this serves to keep the wolves at bay. However ... the times they are a changin'.

Even in Jesus' time there was a church safety team. It was called the temple guard. According to jewishencyclopedia. com:

> *"A strict watch over the Temple was maintained, the guard being composed of three priests and twenty-one Levites. The priests were stationed one at the Chamber of the Flame ("Bet ha-Niẓoẓ"), one at the Chamber of the Hearth ("Bet ha-Moḳed"), and one at the Chamber (attic) of Abṭinas. The Levites kept guard as follows: one at each of the five gates of the mount entrances; one at each of the four corners within the mount enclosure; one at each of the five important gates of the courts; one at each of the four corners within the court; one at the Chamber of Sacrifice; one at the Chamber of Curtains; and one behind the "Kapporet" (Holy of Holies). The captain of the guard saw that every man was alert, chastising a priest if found asleep at his post, and sometimes even punishing him by burning his shirt upon him, as a warning to others (Mid. i. 1)."*

That sounds pretty serious to me. If you go to the state of Israel today, you'll discover that the Jews have become even more serious about safety. It is not unusual to see armed soldiers on street corners and in buildings. Every capable citizen over the age of 18 is required to be trained and serve in the military.

I believe that Israel is a picture of the world's future.

Terrorism and lawlessness is on the rise as we extend into the last days. Disagree at your own peril.

But what can you do if your pastor or governing body refuses to allow an armed church safety team? Certainly you must submit to their authority. However, that doesn't mean you have to sit down, shut up and be good little boys and girls. To the contrary, you should be sounding the battle cry, tolling the clarion call for common sense and protection. You just have to do it in a nice way, in a Godly way, a respectful way, in a way that convinces those around you that it's the right thing to do, and that you are the voice of reason.

I serve as a security consultant for quite a few churches as part of my business. I also teach mass shooter threat classes as part of my local Sheriff's Auxiliary. As such, I see a lot of churches with their heads in the sand, refusing to even discuss the possibility that they might not be safe. It is sad to watch, but there is hope on the horizon.

I recently took on a new church. They had been trying to form an armed safety team for three years, and just now succeeded in getting the blessing of the church body. One of the stipulations was they must take 8 hours of basic pistol training, 8 hours of advanced tactical training, and also qualify on the range using the FBI standard qualification test. I was honored to train and qualify them.

Here are some recommendations to follow if your church is resisting your attempts to form an armed safety team:

Start out with an unarmed safety team.

Organize the safety team as a ministry, because that's what it is. You are responsible for the physical safety of everyone who sets foot onto your property, just as others are responsible to minister to the spiritual needs of church-goers. Your ministry is important for one simple reason:

If you can't keep your parishioners alive, then the pastor cannot minister to their souls. Because of this, you need to take a comprehensive approach to church safety by planning for the following threats:

Medical emergencies

Your team should include people trained in first aid, CPR and AED operations. AED and CPR are not that hard to do, provided you have the training, and you can get that training in less than a day. AED training is simple, and you can find a class in your area by going to the American Red Cross at www.redcross.org. The same is true for first aid and CPR training.

Store your AED (Automated External Defibrillator) in a central location, and make sure your team knows where it is and how to use it.

An automated external defibrillator (AED) is a portable electronic device that automatically diagnoses the life-threatening cardiac arrhythmias of ventricular fibrillation and pulseless ventricular tachycardia, and is able to treat them through defibrillation, the application of electricity which stops the arrhythmia, allowing the heart to re-establish an effective rhythm.

wikipedia.org

CPR (Cardiopulmonary Resuscitation) is different than AED.

Cardiopulmonary resuscitation (CPR) is an emergency procedure that combines chest compressions often with artificial ventilation in an effort to manually preserve intact brain function until further measures are taken to

restore spontaneous blood circulation and breathing in
a person who is in cardiac arrest.

wikipedia.org

Ideally, your entire team should be trained in both CPR
and AED techniques. After all, medical emergencies such as
this happen far more often than mass shooting events.

Your church should also have a BLS (Basic Life Support)
kit.

Basic life support (BLS) is a level of medical care which
is used for victims of life-threatening illnesses or inju-
ries until they can be given full medical care at a hos-
pital. It can be provided by trained medical personnel,
including emergency medical technicians, paramedics,
and by qualified bystanders.

wikipedia.org

A BLS will cost two to three hundred dollars. The AED is
more expensive and will run in the neighborhood of twelve to
fifteen-hundred dollars.

If you can't afford anything else, at least get the training.
It runs about thirty dollars for basic first aid and CPR classes.

Communication

Communication is key to protecting your place of worship.
It allows all team members to respond quickly and efficient-
ly and properly to any given emergency. This is especially
true of mid-sized to large churches where team members are
spread out over several buildings. In the small church, simply yell and anyone can hear you, but in the larger church,
electronic communications will be necessary. I've seen this
accomplished in several ways:

- Family Service Radios - These are affordable and provide instant communication to all team members. You can use them with or without ear buds, depending on the needs of your church. Larger churches with bigger budgets may want to purchase better quality radios.

- Cell phones - This requires no purchase as everyone already has a cell phone. You can communicate via text or phone, but it will not be as instant as the radio.

- Display codes - Typically, a numeric code will be displayed on the screen in the auditorium and/or each room. Each code has a specific meaning, and all team members and volunteers will respond in accordance with their training.

- Surveillance Cameras - These are surprisingly affordable through wireless security companies like SimpliSafe.com. For hundreds of dollars, you can install cameras outside and inside your building at key points. These cameras can be accessed at a central computer, or remotely accessed through your cell phone.

Fire Safety

Chances are you already have this up and running in your church, but you should check and confirm the following:

- All fire extinguishers are charged and operational and up to code.

- Emergency exits are not blocked and are operational.

- Ensure your emergency contact list is up to date and clearly posted.

- Your church floor plan is up to date and clearly posted.

- Evacuation plans are up to date and clearly posted.

• Once a year check for burned out bulbs in your emergency lighting.

• Make sure exterior trash containers are placed away from building to discourage arson.

• Make sure that space heaters are up to code and used at least three feet away from flammable items.

Run through the above safety checklist at least once a year. It's also a good idea to invite your local fire chief to walk through your church and look for anything that is a fire hazard or not up to code. Many times a local fire department will review your fire safety procedures and work with you to improve them.

Adverse Weather

Tornadoes, hurricanes, and severe thunderstorms are a cause for concern, and vary in frequency, depending on your location. But they are very real and life-threatening concerns for churches. The safety team should ensure that all parishioners are informed and updated on any severe weather activity in your area during a church activity.

It's a good idea to have a weather alert radio in your church, and make sure it is turned on and functioning properly during services. You can also upload free weather alert apps to your cell phone from places like NOAA or The Weather Channel. These are free tools and a must-have for all safety team members.

Most importantly, you should have written procedures for how you are going to handle severe weather conditions which are common in your area. The procedures should be clearly posted and disseminated to all safety team members as well as teachers, ushers and other staff members.

Child Protection Policy

These days it's a must to have policies in place that protect our children from child predators and other not-so-obvious threats. With a divorce rate in excess of fifty percent, even the smallest of rural churches will experience problems with parental custody issues, such as one parent taking the child when it isn't lawful for him to do so.

If possible, locate the nursery and Sunday School classes in a location that is not readily accessible to the outside. Your church should be set up with several concentric rings of security, with the children protected in your innermost circle.

You will also need written procedures for dropping off and picking up the children. All workers and parents must be clearly educated on the system, and it must be followed to the letter. This is an important issue of child safety and church liability.

For mid-sized and larger churches, I advise you to assign a dedicated safety team member to the children's area.

Policies and Procedures

Every church should have a complete set of written procedures on how to handle all these emergencies and safety issues. Procedures should be reviewed and updated on a quarterly basis. All written procedures should be clearly posted in every room of the church, and every volunteer and staff member should be formally trained as to their implementation.

As a minimum, you should include the following procedures:

- In case of severe weather
- In case of fire

- In case of armed threat
- In case of unarmed physical threat
- In case of bomb threat
- In case of gas leak
- In case of suicide
- In case of verbal and unruly subject
- In case of medical assistance needed

In this present age of violence and litigation, it is important that all churches have complete and updated policies and procedures on hand to protect them from physical harm and from liability damage.

Things to Remember

1. Church safety has always been an issue, and is documented in the Bible.

2. Your job on the safety team is to protect everyone who enters church property from all manner of physical harm.

3. The Safety Team should be viewed as a regular part of church ministry. It is your calling to serve God and His people.

4. You may meet great opposition to arming your safety team from others inside your church. Be patient and wise.

5. Take a comprehensive approach to forming your safety team. Start with non-controversial issues like medical, fire, child safety, weather, and then build on that foundation.

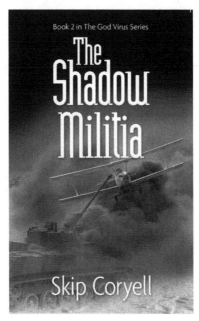

Six months earlier in, *The God Virus,* the lights went out across America, throwing our country into turmoil and chaos, unleashing the demons of a million souls upon an unsuspecting humanity. Dan Branch and his family, caught in the meat grinder of societal collapse, battled their way back home, only to find a new and greater threat waiting for them. Once again, Dan and his family must fight for survival against impossible odds. But this time they are not alone. Their enemy is powerful and cruel, but now Dan is joined by an even greater source of good, evening the odds and giving them a fighting chance. As the Golden Horde marches toward them, leaving death, suffering and destruction in its path, *The Shadow Militia* takes charge!

"I'm a sheepdog. I live to protect the flock and confront the wolf. If you have no capacity for violence then you are a healthy productive citizen, a sheep. If you have a capacity for violence and no empathy for your fellow citizens, then you have defined an aggressive sociopath, a wolf. But what if you have a capacity for violence, and a deep love for your fellow citizens? What do you have then? A sheepdog, a warrior, someone who is walking the hero's path. Someone who can walk into the heart of darkness, into the universal human phobia, and walk out unscathed."

—LTC(RET) Dave Grossman, RANGER, Ph.D., author of "On Killing."—

Chapter 13

The Mass Shooter Threat

I **AM TALKING TO THE SHEEPDOGS NOW.**
The warriors. Snowflakes and wussies may now leave the room with their tails tucked neatly between their back legs. We are going to talk about stopping active shooters, and this could get real messy. So, if you are faint of heart or don't have a strong stomach, then go on ... get out while you still can. Go back to watching *Oprah* and reruns of *Gilligan's Island*.

However, if you're tired of living in fear, grazing like a sheep, living day to day, outsourcing your own personal protection to complete strangers, then ... okay ... you can stay. Buckle up, warrior, cuz here we go!

Who is this guy?

The FBI defines the active shooter as:

> "An individual actively engaged in killing or attempting to kill people in a confined and populated area."

That's the enemy. That's the guy you're going to be stopping. But what does the enemy look like. How will you know him when you see him?

> *"If you know the enemy and know yourself, you need not fear the result of a hundred battles. If you know yourself but not the enemy, for every victory gained you will also suffer a defeat. If you know neither the enemy nor yourself, you will succumb in every battle."*

> — *Sun Tzu, The Art of War*

According to information on statista.com, mass shooters will look like this: (The following data results from analysis done on 110 mass shootings carried out between 1982 and 2019.)

- They will overwhelmingly be male. (107 of the 110 mass shooters were male.)
- 62 of the 110 mass shooters were white.
- Most will kill with handguns.

Wow, so it's not looking real good for white guys. But statistics don't tell the whole story. It's not that easy. Sixty percent of the US population are Caucasian, so it makes sense that whites would comprise the majority of the mass shootings, since they comprise the majority of the population.

But why so many men? Well, I did some extensive online research about that, and here's what all the experts seem to say:

They don't know for sure.

They have plenty of theories, ranging from too much testosterone to lack of nurturing to video game desensitization all the way to angry men trying to regain their lost place at the top of the world pecking order. Pick one or none or pick all of them. But in the end, how much does it matter? My job in this chapter isn't to analyze the mass shooter, but to encourage you and give you information that will help you stop the threat.

So, in the end, all you need to know is that he'll be a he, which means he'll have the strength and aggression associated with most males in our society.

As to why he's trying to kill as many people as possible before shooting himself ... how much does that matter? Most agree that the person is mentally ill, though not necessarily diagnosed or treated as ill. Most agree he feels slighted by society or life in general. But again, none of this matters when he walks into your church and starts killing people.

Think about it this way. When a man walks up to you on the street and points a gun in your face and says "I'm going to kill you." At that point in time, do you really care about his potty training, his upbringing or his emotional state? Probably not. If you do, then you're a more compassionate person than I am. For me, at that point in time, right before he pulls the trigger ... I don't care about "why." I care about "How." As in "How am I going to stop this guy from killing me and everyone else in sight."

How do I stop this guy?

You've probably heard the phrase:

> *"The only way to stop a bad guy with a gun,*
> *is with a good guy with a gun."*

That phrase is very catchy, and most people in the pro-gun community love to espouse it, however, that phrase simply isn't true. This phrase is more accurate:

> *"The **best** way to stop a bad guy with a gun,*
> *is with a good guy with a gun."*

Now, don't get me wrong, I'm a staunch advocate of legally-armed and well trained citizens, not just in church, but all over America. I wouldn't be caught dead without a gun in a church. (No pun intended.) According to the stats:

> *"While 74 percent of mass shootings*
> *occurred in gun free zones, those shootings*
> *were responsible for 85 percent of the*
> *deaths, or 379 of 448 murders."*

> *Michael Martin, Countering the Mass*
> *Shooter Threat*

It is my own personal policy (rule) to never enter a gun-free zone unless I absolutely have to. Why? Because I don't want to have to take out a mass shooter with only my bare hands. Taking away my gun doesn't really promote a fair fight now does it. There's nothing that angers me more than taking a perfectly good warrior, someone with the ability and mindset and skills to protect and defend, and disarming him just so the rest of the sheep can "feel" safe. (And let me point out here that "feeling safe" isn't the same as "being safe".)

Can I take out the shooter with my bare hands?

To that I answer a clarified "yes."

I can, but it sure is a lot harder and a lot more dangerous, not to mention my chances of success go down exponentially when my gun is locked up in my car, instead of on my hip where it belongs. Yes, I can form a team and use swarming tactics to stop the threat. Yes, I can break off a broom handle and try to beat him senseless. Yes, I can rush him and stab him in the eye with an ink pen, but ... now follow me closely here ... isn't it a lot easier and more effective just to shoot the gentleman in the face? I mean, really. Am I being too harsh to suggest that warriors should have weapons; that lions should have teeth; that eagles should have claws?

Okay, so you'll need a gun. Along with that, you'll want to answer a few questions:

What kind of gun is best?

The majority of the people I teach in concealed carry classes show up with a gun they have no intention of carrying. Truth is, most of them will never carry a gun, because they are just checking off boxes so they can "feel" safe. The same is true for many armed safety team members.

In the training I hold for them, they show up with a full-frame pistol, one that shoots very well, and is fairly accurate. And they carry it in an easily accessible outside-the waistband (OWB) holster. That's a good choice, but here's the problem. That's not the gun they carry in church. When working church safety, they carry a compact gun in an inside-the-waistband (IWB) holster. That's like comparing apples and oranges. The two are not the same.

Any gun will never out-shoot its capabilities, and the larger gun (all other things being equal) will always be more accurate than the smaller gun. It will also have less felt recoil, be easier to draw, and have a higher magazine capacity. Those are all great attributes in a gunfight.

So, why do people choose the smaller gun over the larger one? For a couple reasons:

1. They do not expect to get into a gun fight. Once again it goes back to "feeling" safe as opposed to "being" safe. They don't really believe they'll ever have to use the gun, so any old gun will do. It's just there to make you feel good, kind of like the Teddy bear you had when you were a kid, or like the favorite blanket of a five-year-old child. They are "probably" right. They will probably never get into a gun fight. But if that's your premise "I'll never get in a gun fight" then why carry a gun at all? Do not base your carry decisions on your emotions. This is a life-or-death matter. Assume that you are going to get in a gun fight, and plan accordingly. Everywhere I go, I plan on a gun fight. I am armed and I'm alert, always expecting the unexpected, and ready at a moment's notice to launch into action. In my mind, it's not a question of "if," but a question of "when." Here are the unvarnished facts: the longer the barrel, the more accurate the gun is capable of shooting. Smaller guns are not designed for long-distance accuracy; they are designed as an anti-mugging device at arm's-length distances. Church safety team members may have to take longer shots. The best place to interdict the mass shooter is in the parking lot before he is inside the shooting gallery. That means a much longer shot. All church safety team members should be accurate out to 75 feet, as a minimum. That means practice and advanced training, as well as a gun that is de-

signed for long-distance accuracy.

2. Many people choose comfort over functionality. In the minds of many people, the gun is an afterthought, and they put it on in the morning like deodorant or cologne. This is a serious issue, and should be treated as such. You are on the church safety team to save lives, not to be comfortable. If you want comfort, stay home in your recliner, sipping on tea and watching television. True warriors sacrifice for the ones they are sworn to protect. And that means putting up with a bit of discomfort.

3. Many people want a smaller gun that is easier to conceal. This again, is a comfort concern, but also a political one. Churches are incredibly political animals and will split off based on the silliest things like, what color to paint the nursery or whether or not to pave the parking lot. The gun you carry shouldn't be based on comfort or politics; it should be based on functionality alone. Does it make me more accurate? Does it make the people around me safer?

In short, your job is to run toward the gun fire, to engage and neutralize an armed attacker as quickly as possible. The best tool for that is a full-sized pistol. Time is of the essence, and every time you hear a gunshot, assume that someone just died. You won't have time to go get a better gun. What you have on you is what you'll be using.

Carry the gun you are most accurate with, and that has a high magazine capacity. That is the best tool for the job.

Things to Remember

1. Stay alert. Always assume that today is the day of your gun fight.

2. It doesn't matter why they are killing people; it matters that you stop them.

3. A mass shooter is an individual actively engaged in killing or attempting to kill people in a confined and populated area.

4. Your job is to run towards the danger and neutralize the threat.

5. Practice at longer distances of 75 feet and more. Interdict the mass shooter in the parking lot if possible.

6. A larger pistol is more accurate than a smaller pistol, and also has a larger magazine capacity.

Faith Based Security Network

If you are a member of a church safety team, you need to check out the Faith Based Security Network (FBSN). You can find out all about them by going to fbsnamerica.com. FBSN was created by Carl Chinn and is a helpful tool and resource for church safety teams all across America.

Carl is no stranger to church safety. In 1996 he was a responder in a standoff with an angry gunman who took hostages at the Focus on the Family ministry. Following the attacker's trial, Chinn began researching and writing on the subject of criminal and other incidents in North American ministries. In 2005, he and others began to develop an intentional security program for New Life Church in Colorado Springs, CO. He was one of the team of responders who engaged the killer on 12/09/2007.

Chinn now speaks to faith-based operators and law-enforcement groups on the subject of lessons learned in ministry security.

Anxiety weighs down the heart, but a kind word cheers it up.

Proverbs 12:25 (NIV)

Chapter 14

A Smile and a Kind Word

CAN YOU REMEMBER ALL THE WAY back to 1972? I was only 14 years old back then, and one of my favorite television shows was *Kung Fu*, starring David Carradine. In the series, Kwai Chang Caine is a Shaolin Monk who killed the Chinese emperor's nephew and is forced to flee China. He came to the American wild west, and for the next three TV seasons, he is chased by bounty hunters and bad men all over the territories. The show was fascinating to me as a young teen, but now I can't stand to watch it, as it's very simplistic and predictable.

The plot line was always the same. Kwai Chang Caine, affectionately known as Grasshopper by his Shaolin master, would be ridiculed and teased by bullies. So Caine would take the abuse silently, sometimes for days on end without a break. But Caine was a pacifist, so he rarely said anything other than "I have no wish to fight you." To be honest with you, I watched the show simply because I knew that Caine would, in the end, kick the snot out of all the bad guys. I loved it and my 14-year-old psyche just feasted on the violence. I remember I used to go downstairs after the show and practice being Caine. I would kick the wall, the chairs, the freezer, anything that got in my way. On more than one occasion I got in trouble for breaking things. More than anything, when I grew up, I wanted to be a karate master.

I wanted to take martial arts, but I didn't know anything about them, other than what I'd learned from David Carradine on television. I recall a man from the neighborhood, whom I respected very much, so I went to him and asked him a very simple but sincere question. "What is the best form of self-defense?" His answer was very simple, but also very disappointing to an impressionable and stupid young boy.

His short answer was: "A kind word."

I remember thinking "That's the dumbest thing I've ever heard. That's crazy!" So I rejected his advice, and never gave it another thought until about age 34 when I was going through my first divorce. It was during that time when I was most tempted to hate another person. I'd lost my kids, my wife, my house, most of my wage, and I was living hand-to-mouth for several years after that. I wanted so much to give myself over to hate, to blame, even to revenge.

I struggled with it for a long time. Finally, I learned that you can't hurt the mother of your children without also hurting your children as well. And I loved my children immeasurably. In the end, I decided to get down on my knees and pray that God would bless my ex-wife. The prayer went like this:

"Dear God. Please bless the labor of her hands. Help her to succeed in all she does. Bless her spiritually, mentally, emotionally and physically. Amen."

It was hard for me to pray that, because my heart wasn't really in it, and it ran counter to my feelings. But every day, for a very long time, I got down on my knees, in private, and I prayed aloud for her. And I'll be darned if God didn't answer that prayer. At first I was a bit miffed. Of all the prayers to answer, God had to choose that one! And then I noticed something. The more God blessed my ex-wife, the better off my children became. And that made it all worthwhile.

> *43 "You have heard that it was said, 'Love your neighbor and hate your enemy.' 44 But I tell you, love your enemies and pray for those who persecute you, 45 that you may be children of your Father in heaven. He causes his sun to rise on the evil and the good, and sends rain on the righteous and the unrighteous.*

> *Matthew 5:43-45 (NIV)*

My ex-wife, in my mind, was my enemy. After all, she did take many steps to hurt me. And not once, but over and over again. I'd always been under the impression that to forgive someone who was still hurting you was foolish, but I learned the opposite, that to forgive your enemy was what God wanted me to do.

> *"But to you who are listening I say: Love your enemies, do good to those who hate you,*

> *Luke 6:27 (NIV)*

So how does this apply to you and I in the realm of self-defense. That's easy. In today's world we get many opportunities for forgiveness. We are slighted and abused almost on a daily basis, both by strangers and by people we love.

One thing I've noticed is this:

> *It is easier to forgive an enemy than to*
> *forgive a friend.*
>
> *William Blake*

And that is so true. When a stranger wrongs me, then it's much easier for me to just let it run off me like water on a duck's back, but ... not so with a friend. I have higher standards for my friends. There are emotions involved because I've come to believe that they love me; and that changes everything.

Anger is usually a secondary emotion. When someone we love wrongs us or betrays us, our first response isn't anger ... it's pain. So we lash out in some way or say things we come to regret later on. It's the hurt that's talking, and the recipient should take it with a grain of salt.

A wise man once said to me:"No matter what happens to you, no matter what people say to you, you should always consider their motives to be at least 10 percent positive."

I can't always do that, but when I do, things usually work out better. Here's an example of how it might work:

Insult - "Skip, you are the ugliest man I've ever seen!"

Response - "Why thank you for noticing that about me."

In my experience, answering an insult with a kind word is disarming to your attacker. And this technique is even easier when dealing with people you don't know.

Let's use road rage as an example. It's quite a common occurrence on America's highways to be honked at or flipped off or insulted in some way. But here's the key:

"It's not personal."

After all, how can it be personal? They're strangers. They don't even know you. When you are being wrongly attacked, try to remember this maxim:

> *"It's not a statement about me; it's a*
> *statement about them."*

Once I realized that insults from strangers weren't personal attacks on me, then it became much easier to answer them with kindness. After all, angry people are seldom happy people, and they are in great need of our prayers and our pity. Jesus commanded us to do this, and He wouldn't have ordered it if it wasn't possible.

> *28 bless those who curse you, pray for those*
> *who mistreat you.*
>
> *Luke 6:28 (NIV)*

Now don't get me wrong, I haven't perfected this "kind-word-thing yet, and I probably never will. However, we are encouraged and directed to at least try. My experience is this: most people respond positively to a kind word, even after they've insulted us.

I'm reminded of President Abraham Lincoln's closing words in his first inaugural address:

> *"I am loath to close. We are not enemies,*
> *but friends. We must not be enemies. Though*
> *passion may have strained it must not break*
> *our bonds of affection. The mystic chords*
> *of memory, stretching from every battlefield*
> *and patriot grave to every living heart and*
> *hearthstone all over this broad land, will yet*
> *swell the chorus of the Union, when again*
> *touched, as surely they will be, by the better*
> *angels of our nature."*

President Lincoln was speaking to the South, those who would soon be deadly enemies. Granted, it didn't work in this case, however, he did try, and that's all God is commanding us to do.

All of us should continue to appeal to the better nature of our angels, not just when people are nice to us, but when people insult us and ridicule us ... especially when they insult us.

Now, at age 61, when I look back at the foolishness of my youth, it's easy to laugh at the way I was, the way I idolized Kwai Chang Caine and the simplistic plots and stories. Over the years of pain and suffering, I've come to realize that a kind word does more than protect us physically; more importantly it also protects our hearts and minds ... the better nature of our angels.

Responding to an insult with a kind word can make both you, and your enemy, a better person.

> *"We often give our enemies the means for our own destruction."*
>
> *Aesop*

Things to Remember

1. Always appeal to the better nature of your enemies.

2. A kind word goes a long way in de-escalating the anger of your enemy.

3. When we return an insult with an insult, then we are no longer part of the solution ... we are part of the problem.

4. Praying for your enemies can change them for the better. More importantly it will make you a better person with a better heart.

> *7 The older counselors replied, "If you are good to these people and do your best to please them and give them a favorable answer, they will always be your loyal subjects."*
>
> *2 Chronicles 10:7 (NLT)*

> Pride goes before destruction, a haughty spirit before a fall.
> *Proverbs 16:18 (NIV)*

Chapter 15

The Problem with Ego

ego[ee-goh, eg-oh]
noun, plural e·gos.
"the "I" or self of any person; a person as thinking, feeling, and willing, and distinguishing itself
from the selves of others and from objects of its
thought."

THE WORD IS SO SMALL, JUST three little letters, but who would ever think that nations could rise and fall on a person's ego, that the misuse of it could cause the untimely demise of an other-wise good and rational person?

In fact, if you do a search in the Bible, you will not find the word "ego." In its purest form, it simply means "I" or "self," and there is no negative connotation given to it. In daily us-age, it has come to be associated with excessive pride or self-ishness.

However you define it, ego and guns do not work and play well together. The power of deadly force in the hands of a selfish person is rarely a good thing. For our purposes today, we'll define ego as selfish pride to the detriment of others and ourselves.

Pride, according to Catholic Church Tradition is one of the seven deadly sins. Even though, when you search in the Bible, you'll not find an itemized list of the seven deadly sins, the Bible in its totality, condemns all of them. According to church tradition, the seven deadly sins are:

> *wrath, greed, lust, pride, envy, sloth and gluttony.*

The closest thing to a list of seven deadly sins in the Bible is found in Proverbs:

> *16 There are six things the Lord hates—no, seven things he detests: 17 haughty eyes, a lying tongue, hands that kill the innocent, 18 a heart that plots evil, feet that race to do wrong, 19 a false witness who pours out lies, a person who sows discord in a family.*

> *Proverbs 6:16-19 (NLT)*

haughty[haw-tee]
adjective, haugh·ti·er, haugh·ti·est.
disdainfully proud; snobbish; scornfully arrogant; supercilious:

So why does the Catholic church consider these sins to be deadly? Primarily because they reflect attitudes that lead to other more serious sins. Things like murder, robbery, assault, lying and cheating.

CS Lewis called pride "the great sin." While John RW Stott referred to it as:

"Pride is your greatest enemy, humility is your greatest friend."

John RW Stott

Certainly there's nothing wrong with being proud of a job well done. I would call that a harmless satisfaction. However, selfish pride and ego undoubtedly harm others, and cannot be denied.

I have been involved in several road-rage incidents throughout the years, and can attest to its irrationality. It first happened to me when I was 19 years old. I had my first car, a 1968 Dodge Charger. (That's right, one of those Dukes of Hazzard cars.) I was on a country road and had moved into the left lane to pass the car ahead of me. The driver sped up, not allowing me to pass. Instead of backing off, I took it personal and sped up as well. He also increased his own speed. By now we are traveling uphill, on a blind curve, and it is now a no-passing lane. At any moment another car could have come from the opposite direction and hit me head on. The smart thing to do would have been to step on the brakes and de-escalate the whole affair. But I wasn't smart. I was young and dumb and full of pride. I rammed the accelerator to the floor and finished passing the car to my right. At the top of the hill, at the next stop sign. I stopped my car and waited for the car behind me to catch up. It didn't take long.

The old man was about 75 years old and he cussed me out something fierce. As it turns out, sometimes stupidity comes in pairs and is no respecter of age. After exchanging unChrist-like words, we both drove away, and, fortunately, never saw each other again.

Now, as a 61-year-old man, I can't believe I was ever that stupid and out of control. But I was, and there are a lot of people out there who never grow up, who live their entire lives, willing to die for the sake of a bruised ego.

At that moment in time, I was so enraged, fueled by ego and pride, that I was willing to die and even kill another person so that an old man's car didn't get the best of me. That seems like the height of foolishness. And yet ... I am still controlled to some degree by my own ego and pride.

There are times, when my ego is bruised, that I get so angry that I want to lash out, honk my horn, flip people off, tap on my brakes, and flail my arms at them in protest. I suppose a part of me will never completely grow up. And maybe that's why self-control is one of the fruits of the spirit ... because we need it so much.

Have you ever gotten an email from someone who bruised your ego? Maybe you asked someone for a favor and they refused, saying that they were just too busy to help you out. That happened to me just a few minutes ago while I was writing this chapter. At first, I felt hurt; then I felt angry; then I wanted to retaliate.

And now I am laughing at myself. Why? Because here I am, the wise one, the one writing the books, giving others advice on how to live their lives, and I can't even take my own wise counsel. The phrase that comes to my mind right now is "What a piece of work!" And so I have to smile and shake my head at how powerful pride really is.

The problem is this: selfish pride and vanity never seem to totally ever be defeated. In fact, the more successful I am, the more my pride seems to slip in and control my thoughts and feelings.

When I think about it, I come to realize that one of the pillars of Christianity is the opposite of pride. It is humility and self-sacrifice.

Where does real humility lead us. The book of Proverbs gives us a simple answer:

> *4 True humility and fear of the Lord lead to riches, honor, and long life.*
>
> *Proverbs 22:4 (NLT)*

The more I read the Bible, the more I realize that humility, honor and wisdom seem to be inextricably linked:

> *33 Fear of the Lord teaches wisdom; humility precedes honor.*
>
> *Proverbs 15:33 (NLT)*

> *12 Haughtiness goes before destruction; humility precedes honor.*
>
> *Proverbs 18:12 (NLT)*

> *23 Pride ends in humiliation, while humility brings honor.*
>
> *Proverbs 29:23 (NLT)*

After all, look at the work of Jesus on the cross. Was that not the most humble of acts in all recorded history? And why exactly did Christ die for us? It certainly was not selfish. It was one of the most painful and self-sacrificial acts ever done.

> *15 He died for everyone so that those who receive his new life will no longer live for themselves. Instead, they will live for Christ, who died and was raised for them.*
>
> *2 Corinthians 5:15 (NLT)*

Read that carefully. Christ died so that we will no longer

live for ourselves. Christ did not die to save our egos ... He died to save us "from" our egos. The pursuit of self (ego) is antithetical to everything that Jesus lived and died and rose again for.

There are some things worth living for:

My faith, my wife, my children, my friends, even a stranger. And, ironically enough, the same things worth living for are also the things worth dying for. But selfish pride and vain ambition are not on this list. Neither traits are worth living or dying for.

> *16 For wherever there is jealousy and selfish ambition, there you will find disorder and evil of every kind.*

> *James 3:16 (NLT)*

When we become Christians, we die to ourselves and become alive in Christ. We no longer live for our own accomplishments. We don't live for fame or wealth or personal success. When I die and stand before our judge, God will not ask me how many friends I had on FaceBook or whether any of my books were New York Times bestsellers. God won't even be impressed with the Pulitzer Prize.

> *3 Don't be selfish; don't try to impress others. Be humble, thinking of others as better than yourselves. 4 Don't look out only for your own interests, but take an interest in others, too. 5 You must have the same attitude that Christ Jesus had.*

> *Philippians 2:3-5 (NLT)*

And if you really live as Christ did, what would it look like in your everyday life? In your everyday concealed carry life?

For example:

A car cuts you off on the highway. How should you respond? Would Jesus flip him off? Would Jesus Christ shake His fist and cuss him out? No. And neither should I. If I truly am living a humble, spirit-filled life, then I should have compassion for the person and pray for them. Can I always do that? That's a big no. But I should at least try my best. I should control my anger and selfish pride.

From a practical point of view, even if you're not a Christian, it is never in your own best interest to respond negatively to rude people. The moment you begin carrying a gun for personal defense, you should become the most polite person on the planet. All your interactions with others should be viewed, not through the prism of self, but with an eye for helping the other person do the right thing. You should always try to de-escalate a verbal confrontation. That's why Jesus commanded us to turn the other cheek when insulted.

Here's my rule of thumb: Every morning when I strap on my firearm, I take the gun out of the safe, put it in my holster, then I reach into my heart, rip out my ego and lock it inside the gun safe.

And that's a rule that we all can live with.

Things to Remember

1. Ego and guns do not mix.

2. Jesus died for us so that we can live our lives for Him, by considering others better than ourselves.

3. Always de-escalate a verbal confrontation.

4. A bruised ego is not worth killing for; neither is it worth dying for.

"There is nothing noble in being superior to your fellow man; true nobility is being superior to your former self."

— *Ernest Hemingway*

Skip is the creator and host of *The Home Defense Show*, a weekly 1-hour podcast about all things home, family and personal defense.

The Home Defense Show podcast is now available on iTunes, Google Play, Spreaker and Sticher. You can also find it on my YouTube channel. This should make it easier than ever for you to listen to my sweet angelic voice coming to you from deep inside the bowels of a great big empty. Don't forget to subscribe. For more info go to homedefenseshow.com

*17 As iron sharpens iron,
so one person sharpens
another.*

Proverbs 27:17 (NIV)`

Chapter 16

Final Words

As I LOOK BACK ON MY LIFE, I KEEP thinking ... I was expecting to be smarter than I am right now. I thought I'd have more money. In my younger days I was convinced that I'd write a best seller and win the Pulitzer prize. Now, at age 61, I'm reminded of the unexpected twists and turns that life can take. In the immortal words of Forrest Gump:

> "Life is like a box of chocolates. Ya never know what yer gonna get."

But I can't deny, that even though there have been some real surprises, some major setbacks, and more than my share of heart ache – all in all ... it's been a good life. A tough life, but good, nonetheless.

I am not a theological man. I don't care much for details. When people talk about theology; they call it discourse. I call it a boring waste of my time. I'm not a big detail person. Take eschatology for example.

eschatology[es-kuh-tol-uh-jee]
noun Theology.
any system of doctrines concerning last, or final, matters, as death, the Judgment, the future state, etc.
the branch of theology dealing with such matters.

Eschatology interests me as a concept, and it's important to me that it happens, but ... the time line, the details of when Jesus comes back for us isn't important to me. It's not important that I know exactly "when" Jesus is coming back; it's important that I know whether or not He's coming back. I don't need the details, and I don't want them. (Reference back to chapter 3, "For I am a bear of very little brain, and long words bother me.") Actually, long words give me a headache, and so does arguing over theology.

It reminds me of one of my favorite movies *Office Space* by Mike Judge. There's a scene in the movie where the main character, Peter Gibbons, is being interviewed to decide whether or not his job will be phased out.

> *"Peter Gibbons: The thing is, Bob, it's not that I'm lazy, it's that I just don't care.*
>
> *Bob Porter: Don't... don't care?*
>
> *Peter Gibbons: It's a problem of motivation, all right? Now if I work my butt off and Initech ships a few extra units, I don't see another dime; so where's the motivation?*

When it comes to the end times, I know what the Bible says about it, because I've been listening to religious people talk about it in great detail since I was a child. Theology in general is like that for me. I care about core doctrine. I care that Jesus loves me. I care that He came down from heaven, sacrificed Himself on the cross and died for my sins so that I won't go to hell. That's important to me. I get it. I need to know that. But the day He's coming back? I don't need to know that. I'm not motivated to try and figure that out.

Whether Jesus comes back for us today or tomorrow or next century; it doesn't matter. That knowledge has no practical value to me. It won't and shouldn't change how I live my day-to-day life. When it comes to theology, here's what I need to know.

> *16 For God so loved the world that he gave his one and only Son, that whoever believes in him shall not perish but have eternal life.*
>
> *John 3:16 (NIV)*

And when it comes to eschatology, I just need to cling to the promise of Jesus:

> *3 And if I go and prepare a place for you, I will come back and take you to be with me that you also may be where I am.*
>
> *John 14:3 (NIV)*

Now, both my wife and my pastor are cringing right now. They are wondering: What's wrong with Skip? How can he not care about the details of theology? Now, I love my wife and my pastor, and they love me as well. But they both come from an engineering background. They love details. I hate them. I shun them. I avoid them like the plague. Don't get me wrong here. I want them both to be the way they are. I want someone to care about the details, I just don't want it to be me.

Another of my favorite movies is the *Matrix* series with Keanu Reeves. In *The Matrix Reloaded*, Neo (played by Keanu Reeves) is speaking with Councillor Harmann (played by Anthony Zerbe). They are discussing the fate of Zion in light of the pending attack by the machines.

> *Councillor Harmann : Down here,*
> *sometimes I think about all those people still*
> *plugged into the Matrix and when I look at*
> *these machines I... I can't help thinking that*
> *in a way... we are plugged into them.*
>
> *Neo : But we control these machines; they*
> *don't control us.*
>
> *Councillor Harmann : Of course not. How*
> *could they? The idea is pure nonsense. But...*
> *it does make one wonder... just... what is*
> *control?*
>
> *Neo : If we wanted, we could shut these*
> *machines down.*
>
> *Councillor Harmann : [Of] course. That's*
> *it. You hit it. That's control, isn't it? If*
> *we wanted we could smash them to bits.*
> *Although, if we did, we'd have to consider*
> *what would happen to our lights, our heat,*
> *our air...*
>
> *Neo : So we need machines and they need*
> *us, is that your point, Councilor?*

*Councillor Harmann: No. No point. Old
men like me don't bother with making points.
There's no point.*

*Neo: Is that why there are no young men on
the council?*

Councillor Harmann: Good point.

The good councillor didn't need to know how the machines worked. He just needed to know the reason for their existence; that they would continue to supply the air and water they needed to survive deep inside the bowels of the earth. Of course, this is all a question of perspective. Councillor Harmann doesn't care about the nuts and bolts of the machinery, but the engineer in charge of keeping it running certainly does.

When it comes to personal protection, I care about the details. I need to know what causes a pistol malfunction. I need to know how to clear a jam in case it happens during a firefight. I need to know what motivates criminals, because a better understanding of their motivation will help me protect and defend against my enemy. I need to understand holster systems, magazines, movement during battle as well as the moral and legal application of deadly force.

But the question of "why" in philosophy and everyday life, can drive a man to suicide. While I'm not a fan of theology, I love to study the characters in the Bible. They are all so flawed, and I relate to them.

David was strong ... when he wasn't being weak.

Abraham was a man of faith ... except when he was doubting God.

I like the character of Job. I wish I could talk to him. I

193

would just love to pick that man's brain. Life is suffering. Life is joy. Life is happy. Life is turmoil. It's always a mix of good and bad and rain and sun.

When I look back on my life I have many regrets, but I don't know that I'd change anything. I have made so many terrible mistakes. I've hurt people, both strangers and the ones I love. I've had two bad marriages, both ending in divorce. I've made plenty of mistakes in raising all seven of my children.

But still ... I don't know that I'd change anything. To change my history is to also change my present and my future, and the lives of everyone around me. Besides, if I changed something, I just might screw it up even worse than I did the first time.

My life is the sum total of every decision I've ever made, of every good and decent act, as well as every mistake, miscalculation and horrendous unkindness.

> *"One man's life touches so many others, and when he's not there, it leaves an awfully big hole."*
>
> Clarence the Angel,
> It's a Wonderful Life

So what is my point? *No. No point. Old men like me don't bother with making points. There's no point.*

But I do have some advice, take it or leave it.

> *Do the best you can with what you've got.*

While we are all image-bearers of Christ and valuable to Him, we are not all the same.

> *14 Even so the body is not made up of one part but of many. 15 Now if the foot should*

say, "Because I am not a hand, I do not belong to the body," it would not for that reason stop being part of the body. 16 And if the ear should say, "Because I am not an eye, I do not belong to the body," it would not for that reason stop being part of the body. 17 If the whole body were an eye, where would the sense of hearing be? If the whole body were an ear, where would the sense of smell be? 18 But in fact God has placed the parts in the body, every one of them, just as he wanted them to be.

I Corinthians 12:14-18 (NIV)

Some of us are spiritually strong. Some of us are physically strong. Some of us are blessed with a kind heart. Some with patience, some with wisdom, some with brains. Some of us are great at encouraging one another.

God gave you a talent. Figure out what that is, develop it and do the best you can to advance the Kingdom of God.

Until the next book or radio show, I leave you with this final tidbit: Stay Positive.

Finally, brothers and sisters, whatever is true, whatever is noble, whatever is right, whatever is pure, whatever is lovely, whatever is admirable—if anything is excellent or praiseworthy—think about such things.

Philippians 4:8 (NIV)

Skip Coryell lives with his wife and children in Michigan. He works full time as a professional writer, and *Concealed Carry for Christians* is his fourteenth published book. He is an avid hunter and sportsman, a Marine Corps veteran, and a graduate of Cornerstone University. You can listen to Skip as he co-hosts the syndicated military talk radio show Frontlines of Freedom on frontlinesoffreedom.com. You can also hear his weekly podcast The Home Defense Show at homedefense-show.com

For more details on Skip Coryell, or to contact him personally, go to his website at skipcoryell.com

BOOKS BY SKIP CORYELL

We Hold These Truths

Bond of Unseen Blood

Church and State

Blood in the Streets

Laughter and Tears

RKBA: Defending the Right to Keep and Bear Arms

Stalking Natalie

The God Virus

The Shadow Militia

The Saracen Tide

The Blind Man's Rage

Civilian Combat - The Concealed Carry Book

Jackpine Strong

Concealed Carry for Christians